Millennium Park Chicago

Cheryl Kent

NORTHWESTERN UNIVERSITY PRESS | EVANSTON, ILLINOIS

Northwestern University Press
www.nupress.northwestern.edu

Printed in Canada

Cover and book design by Marianne Jankowski

10 9 8 7 6 5 4 3 2 1

Library of Congress Cataloging-in-Publication Data
Kent, Cheryl.
Millennium Park Chicago / Cheryl Kent.
p. cm.
ISBN 978-0-8101-2682-4 (pbk. : alk. paper)
1. Millennium Park (Chicago, Ill.) 2. Urban parks—Illinois—Chicago. I. Title.
SB466.U7M555 2011
712.50977311—dc22

2010044540

♾ The paper used in this publication meets the minimum requirements of the American National Standard for Information Sciences—Permanence of Paper for Printed Library Materials, ANSI Z39.48-1992.

Contents

EXELON PAVILION

Acknowledgments

I first wrote about Millennium Park for the Arts and Leisure section of the *New York Times* in May 2000, when Frank Gehry's design for the Jay Pritzker Pavilion was unveiled. He told me, charmingly, that his performance structure was "like putting a bouquet of flowers on the table." The prospect of having one of his buildings in Chicago was thrilling and invited thoughts of shaking up a city that had been sitting on its historic architectural laurels for too long.

At the time, I thought—as did everyone else—that Gehry's work would be the pinnacle of Millennium Park. Then came *Cloud Gate* (aka "The Bean"), the Crown Fountain, the Harris Theater, and the Lurie Garden, as the park's sponsors stepped forward one after another to support great work.

Telling the story of Millennium Park's creation has offered moments of pure joy, such as clambering around in the rafters of the Pritzker Pavilion in a brisk winter wind with Ed Uhlir—a key player in making the park happen—as my guide, and getting inside *Cloud Gate* to observe the process of finishing the sculpture's surface and to meet the steelworkers who created the "moment of perfection," as Anish Kapoor calls it. There are few pleasures greater than talking to people who are passionate about their work and are very good at it. I am grateful to the scores of people who granted me interviews for this book. The help of Ed Uhlir and John Bryan in obtaining these interviews was invaluable, as were the hours they spent talking to me.

This book would not have been possible without the generosity of the photographers whose images, as beautiful and hard-won as anything in the park itself, appear in the following pages. I am more grateful to them than I can say.

—*Cheryl Kent*

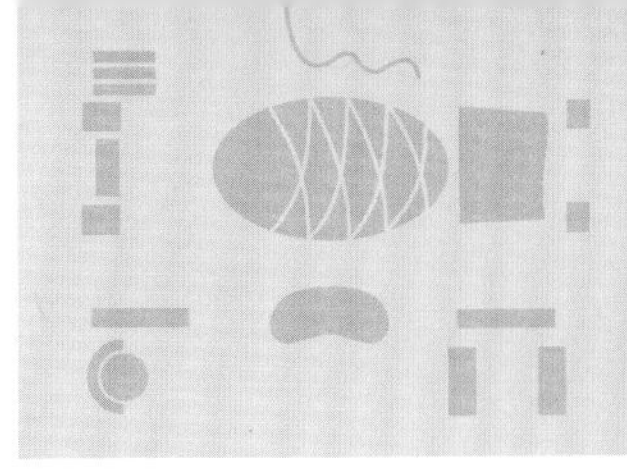

From Nothing: The Story of Millennium Park

Something was about to happen that would elevate Chicago in the eyes of the world.

—JOHN BRYAN

Out of thin air Chicago created Millennium Park in the very heart of the city and in so doing reinvented what a park can be. This is a new urban creature, as much museum, performance hall, and public square as park. Its inspiration follows Chicago's oldest and best traditions, those that left Chicago's lakefront open for public beaches and parks, those that led to the founding of the Art Institute of Chicago by business philanthropists.

Millennium Park is a sophisticated and urbane showcase for contemporary art, architecture, and landscaping. The park stands on a massive, constructed platform—essentially a piece of invented or found land. It spans below-ground rail lines, an express bus lane, and two parking garages. Neighbor to the Chicago Symphony, the Art Institute of Chicago, the Cultural Center, the new Spertus Institute of Jewish Studies, and a solid block of landmark high-rises (including two designed by the world-renowned architect Louis Sullivan), this park is the last urban piece that, once fitted into place, consolidated a cultural zone previously lacking coherence. An open pit of tangled rails and parking—a long-standing eyesore—was turned into a beguiling public space; a place people once avoided now draws them.

This unlikely park emerged from a continuously evolving, sometimes controversial process that resulted in a much larger, dramatically more ambitious project than the one initially conceived. The process was haphazard in some ways, driven (as opposed to directed) by succeeding rounds of bar raising and hurdle clearing. Every time donors and planners thought to do more, they were able to pull it off, which only encouraged them to raise the stakes again.

Was the park's expense worth it? That's a question reasonable people may answer differently. That Millennium Park overcame mediocrity—the greatest inevitable force operating in city planning outside physics—to become an exceptional public space is beyond doubt.

The process's flexibility—or its lack of careful planning, depending on your point of view—ultimately served the park well, allowing skillful and talented people to flourish. Some were left behind as the park expanded, while others did their best work to date at Millennium Park, including Anish Kapoor, the creator of the enormous steel sculpture *Cloud Gate* (affectionately known as "The Bean" by Chicagoans for its shape), and Ethan Silva, who figured out how to build it. Could a park like this have been produced by other means? Had the original master plan included all the elements ultimately built, it would have been shot down—and not without justification—as unrealistic and unaffordable. If nothing else, the number of the park's firsts would have been daunting had they all been included in the plan at the start. Among them must be counted *Cloud Gate,* the Pritzker Pavilion's sound system and trellis, and the Crown Fountain towers. Building anything for the first time is much harder than building it for the hundredth. The return on investment in the first is the efficiency captured in duplication.

LAUGH
STAY
DANCE
LAUGH
STAY
DANCE
PARK GRILL

To put Millennium Park in context, imagine what it would be like if nearly twenty-five acres next door to the Louvre in Paris became a public park; or if Central Park, which wraps behind the Metropolitan Museum in New York, were enlarged by twenty-five acres. And then put these visions out of your mind because they are not going to happen. Land at the center of cities is much easier to imagine as prime tax-generating real estate. But in Chicago's case, the land was more or less invented, and then it was kept off the tax rolls and given to the public. The rarity of the occasion cannot be exaggerated; a mature city has created an important new public space at its center.

Millennium Park is true public space. It is not a retail mall where every giant frosted snowflake and Santa Claus is a calculated come-on to persuade consumers to spend more time and more money. Although the practice has been a source of criticism, pieces such as the BP Bridge, the Chase Promenade, and the Jay Pritzker Pavilion are named for their primary sponsors. That is the nature of philanthropy (anyone who thinks otherwise should visit a Carnegie Library or the Trump ice-skating rink in Central Park). There is no charge for visiting Millennium Park, and the programming is free. Most American museums can claim as much only one day a week. The bulk of the operating and maintenance budget for Millennium Park comes from sources outside tax revenues. In a nation that prizes individualism and that possesses a cultural climate indisposed to support costly civic gestures, Millennium Park is a singularly democratic achievement—an enormously generous gift of art to the public.

The park upends the model of urban renewal in place since the 1970s, when Benjamin Thompson invented the "festival marketplace" with the renovation of Faneuil Hall in Boston. Cities were viewed as dark and dangerous places then, and the flight to suburbs was still on the wing. Architects and planners tried to at once preserve historic sites and soften rough urban edges in order to bring people downtown. The result, as was the case at Navy Pier in Chicago, was usually an isolated carnival in the middle of the city, utterly suburban in feeling and seldom visited by anyone other than tourists. By contrast, Millennium Park celebrates the qualities city dwellers prize about their home: the access it provides to art, music, theater, and culture in general. Without pandering, the best of contemporary art, architecture, and landscape design is offered to the public with full confidence that it will be understood and appreciated.

The measure of success for any public space is its capacity to draw people to it. Millennium Park attracts all sorts, inviting them to mingle and enjoy the coequal gifts bestowed by thriving cities, those of surprise and recognition. Visitors come from all over the world, as well as Chicago and its suburbs. What brings them? Some of them are art and architecture pilgrims. People linger in public to watch one another because we like to recognize human behavior and be surprised by its variations. In every public square—from Piazza San Marco in Venice to Tiananmen Square in Beijing—people will watch small children chasing pigeons because the chasing is as inevitable as it is varied, fruitless, and funny. You don't have to speak Italian or Chinese to enjoy the show and the feeling of belonging it bestows. In Millennium Park, the children playing in Crown Fountain in summer and those ice-skating in winter provide a similar spectacle and its attendant satisfactions.

Like the best parks, Millennium Park epitomizes its age. Built any sooner or later, it would have become something quite different. Just as Frederick Law Olmsted's Central Park (1859) is a fabricated pastoral landscape (there is little that is authentic about that park's topography, convincing though it is) intended as an antidote to the hard, industrial city, Millennium Park is a designed answer to the needs of people in a postindustrial age. And what is it that we need, what are we responding to in Millennium Park? We want mystery and beauty, *Cloud Gate* tells us; we want to interact with our environment, the Crown Fountain demonstrates; we want to be overwhelmed and enveloped, the Pritzker Pavilion says; we want the journey to be a passage, according to the BP Bridge. Above all, the park speaks to the most elemental quality in human character—the need to congregate. In this way, the park serves the traditional democratic function of the public square. There are no soapboxes here, but this is a gathering place for people.

The park extends its reach to important parts of the city along perpendicular axes. The crowds attracted to shopping along North Michigan Avenue are crossing the bridge at the Chicago River now and heading south to Millennium Park, opening this great street more fully. In turn, Michigan Avenue has been connected to Lake Michigan, the city's single gorgeous natural feature, by way of Millennium Park's sinuous pedestrian bridge to Grant Park overlooking the lake. The Loop—Chicago's traditional downtown center, which includes government and commercial buildings—is drawn into the park's orbit as well. The Pritzker Pavilion's billowing steel sails mark the eastern end of Washington Street and can be seen from more than one mile away. This celebratory terminus confers the status this street deserves, containing as it does such important local government institutions as city hall, the county building, and the Daley Center. (The giant Picasso sculpture standing in Daley Plaza on Washington anticipated Millennium Park in one respect: it has been used by generations of Chicago's children as a slide, providing an early demonstration of the way incredibly valuable public art adapts as play equipment.)

So intimately and assuredly has the park been woven into the fabric of the city that it has acquired a sense of inevitability, as though it could not have been developed any other way. This is true only to the degree that it is difficult, even for those who have lived here all their lives, to recall what the site of the park looked like before 2004. There was never anything inevitable about it. The park required extraordinary efforts by many people over many years.

During those years when it was a work in progress, there was no shortage of criticism. Chicago was making something extraordinary, and, even though it was going up right under their noses, the local journalists who covered it—with two notable exceptions: the *Chicago Tribune*'s Pulitzer Prize–winning architecture critic, Blair Kamin, and John McCarron, who wrote a favorable editorial for the *Tribune*—did not "get it" until it was done. "We missed the story," said McCarron, a longtime reporter for the *Tribune* who served on the paper's editorial board and now teaches at Northwestern's Medill School of Journalism.

The missed story McCarron referred to specifically was the collaboration between the private and public sectors. Donors paid for everything other than infrastructure in Millennium Park. Individuals and companies gave more than $235 million to the park, all of it offered and accepted as a gift to the city and its people. In truth, the private-public collaboration had been tested once before when Chicago was named host to the 1996 Democratic National Convention. Private and corporate contributions paid for everything short of police services. Business executives and city leaders were anxious to rejuvenate Chicago's image, replacing the one of rioting burned into the national memory in 1968, the last time the city played host. The success of the fund-raising and the convention itself proved the public-private model could work. Gifts on the scale of Millennium Park are given on occasion to private museums, opera companies, and universities, but to a city government? That is unusual.

The closest comparison is the Central Park Conservancy in New York City, through which philanthropists have assumed 80 percent of the financial responsibility and much of the control of the park after the city showed that it could not care for it. But the preservation of a valuable, profoundly threatened, and beloved resource is substantially different and easier to argue than the invention of something so new it is difficult to describe to anyone who has not seen it. (The conservancy may yet provide a model for the administration of Millennium Park. As the conservancy did, Millennium Park's board is actively raising money for an endowment that would support park maintenance and be overseen by an independent board.)

Legal agreements were drafted and signed by the City of Chicago and the park fundraisers—the organization known as Millennium Park, Inc. (MPI). The donors would be responsible for everything above the surface of the park. The city would be responsible for building the deck and infrastructure. It did not always work out that cleanly and clearly. When infrastructure costs increased, the city turned to revenue sources it had not intended to tap, causing considerable controversy and an unrelenting drumbeat of criticism from the *Chicago Tribune* in particular. Donors also found themselves stretched by unanticipated costs for some of the commissioned pieces, *Cloud Gate* in particular. The legal agreements did, however, give donors confidence that their gifts would be used as intended. For added security, most brought in their own construction managers to oversee the work and, more to the point, to be certain the object of their philanthropy was not co-opted by city politics and processes. The realty and management company US Equities was hired to coordinate the work on *Cloud Gate,* the BP Bridge, Crown Fountain, the Pritzker Pavilion, and the Lurie Garden.

Asked why the collaboration worked, the answer from many sources is the same, and something of a paradox: a strong mayor and the certainty that construction of the park would proceed beyond the reach of city government. John Bryan, the former president and CEO of Sara Lee and former president of the Art Institute's board of directors, who led the fund-raising efforts, said of Mayor Richard M. Daley, "He runs the city in a businesslike way. The fact that we have the mayor we do encourages us." Cindy Pritzker, whose family contributed the largest sum to the park, put it another way: "He gets people together." She means it as a compliment when she adds that Daley, a Democrat, is "really a Republican in drag." Even those who are not fans of the mayor give him credit. "We live under a benign dictatorship," said McCarron.

Still, to win donors' confidence, the park was, to the extent possible, intentionally left outside conventional city processes. Bond sales for the project were approved by the Chicago City Council as required, but the park was never under its control, nor was the council's input solicited. "And aren't we glad about that?" said McCarron, referring to the organization's generally perceived crudeness. Indeed, the rough-edged then alderman Burt Natarus, who represented the district in which the park stands while it was under construction, had no authority over the project and ended up in the audience instead of at the podium for dedication ceremonies.

Bryan, key to the park's conception because of his artistic ambitions for Chicago and his experience raising funds for the 1996 convention, brought in donors and orchestrated their contributions. He had brought in millions for Lyric Opera, and, in his role as president of the board at the Art Institute, he raised money for the addition of the Modern Wing (2009). His efforts on behalf of the arts bring to mind Chicago's great business philanthropists of the 1890s, who created or expanded all of Chicago's major cultural institutions.

City officials put their confidence in the donors, trusting they would select suitable works for a public space. To some degree, that is a pattern in keeping with a long tradition of individuals and private groups contributing to public parks in Chicago and, for that matter, other cities. The German community paid for the Schiller Monument in Lincoln Park, installed in 1885, and Kate Buckingham paid for a fountain dedicated to her brother's memory in Grant Park in 1927. Millennium Park, however, is unique for the scale, concentration, and size of its donations. There were safeguards in place: the donors availed themselves of experts from the Art Institute of Chicago as well as gallery owner Richard Gray and architect John Vinci. But, broadly speaking, constraints were lightly exercised. It was less a formalized approval process in which the city and the donors played equal roles than a fluid process adapted to the circumstances. For the Lurie Garden, there was a formal competition. In the case of the Pritzker Pavilion, Frank Gehry was selected by the donor to be the architect. (The Pritzkers, who are behind one of the most prestigious awards given to architects, were thought to have some authority when it came to choosing architects of quality.) When James Wood, then president of the Art Institute of Chicago, objected to the size of the yet-to-be-built Crown Fountain, a full-scale mockup was constructed to demonstrate that the proportions worked. No one wanted to overplay their hand or draw lines in the sand.

Edward Uhlir, an architect, was crucial to keeping the balance. He was preparing to retire as director of research and planning from the Chicago Park District after a twenty-two-year career when he was drafted by the mayor to oversee the park project. John Bryan,

Mayor Daley, and Uhlir would work closely together throughout the project. Uhlir started working informally on Millennium Park in August 1998, just eighteen weeks after the project was announced.

Shortly after, the park suffered its first public—and avoidable—setback when the deterioration of the aged parking garage underlying the ribbon of park along Michigan Avenue was exposed. What had long been obvious to anyone who used the garage became headline news in 1998: the nearly fifty-year-old garage was falling apart. With some of its support columns shored up by timber and with water coming in, the problems were not subtle. The garage could not possibly support any portion of the proposed deck for Millennium Park and would have to be rebuilt. The Chicago Park District, which had built and operated the garage, would be responsible for financing the new structure with a $72 million bond issue. In the press, however, this development was characterized as an expansion of Millennium Park's budget and a cost overrun. The negative image would prove impossible to shake until the park was completed.

In September, Uhlir's appointment was official. The city's project manager, Ed Bedore, who had actually recommended filling the failing garage with dirt, was gone. Uhlir's contract reflected his position straddling two realms. With the title project director, he was a consultant billing his time both to the city and to the donors' organization, MPI. Uhlir became the key, trusted link between the city and the donors. Together with a deep knowledge of the city, Uhlir also brought his political skills and an understanding of technical structural issues to the job. He was positioned to protect both the city's and the donors' investments, and he supplied the skills and knowledge needed to get the park built. When architects, designers, and artists presented their plans, Uhlir was the only one who could look at them critically, challenge them, and get them fixed.

Rebuilding the garage under Michigan Avenue may have been a public relations fiasco, but in the end it improved the park immeasurably, providing a number of critical opportunities. The old park along Michigan Avenue standing above the garage came into play. It had been a thoroughly uninviting public space, underused and consequently a magnet for vagrants. Originally, a simple sprucing up was planned. The demolition of the old park's foundations meant it could be redesigned and incorporated into Millennium Park, enlarging it by 50 percent, to 24.5 acres. Instead of a back-end piece of Grant Park, Millennium Park became a prominent part of Michigan Avenue, firmly oriented toward the city and linked to many of its most distinguished institutions. The sharp change in levels between Michigan Avenue and the park's deck could be smoothed into a slope that would make the park accessible to persons with disabilities entering from Michigan Avenue. The ugly down ramps to the old garage, which had run right next to the sidewalk on the east side of Michigan Avenue and had kept pedestrians away, could be moved to the center of the street and substantially masked with seasonal plantings. They provide an island for pedestrians crossing Michigan Avenue and a barrier between northbound and southbound traffic.

The numbers coming together were promising. The part the city was building—the parking garages beneath the deck—was to repay its construction costs over time and provide funds to maintain the park. As the complexity of the park and its component pieces grew, however, annual maintenance funds for the park also grew, to an annual cost of $7.4 million in 2006. Parking fees were inadequate, and the city tapped the advertising revenue generated by the bus shelters as the alternative source for Millennium Park's maintenance costs. In 2006, the city signed a 99-year lease deeding management of four downtown garages, including the two at Millennium Park, to Morgan Stanley for $563 million. The cash is being used, in part, to pay off the bonds the city levied to build the park's deck and infrastructure.

The overwhelmingly negative press coverage of Millennium Park during its construction—not all of it unwarranted—did not take into account most of the developments that led to its success. Within one year of its formal announcement in 1998, the space for the park was increased by 50 percent. By 1999, the master plan for the park, by Adrian Smith, then a partner at the prestigious Skidmore, Owings & Merrill (SOM), had been substantially redesigned, no longer calling for a simple Beaux Arts expanse of green. The opening date had changed too; although no one working on the park thought it would be finished in time for the millennium, neither did they think it would take until 2004. A front-page story in the *Tribune,* dated October 30, 2002, finally took up the donors' story under the sardonic headline, "City's Rich Kicking in for Millennium Park." By that time, Bryan had collected $75 million and had been actively fund-raising for more than three years.

John Bryan and Cindy Pritzker, whose family donated the largest gift, of $15 million, did their best to ignore the newspaper stories. At city hall, where those stories carried political implications, that was not an option. Anyone working on the park tried to avoid the tense, obstreperous progress meetings with the mayor. Bryan said, "It never occurred to the news media that something was about to happen that would elevate Chicago in the eyes of the world and raise the spirit of the people and [begin] an economic renaissance in the central part of the city. They didn't write those articles. They couldn't envision it at all." In the end, Bryan believes the nature of the press coverage added to the surprise when the park opened. "I think part of the success of the park came from the low expectations set by the press," he said.

Opening day

With construction still going on the day before the opening, "nobody was paying much attention," said Helen Doria, the park's executive director. "Thursday night the construction fences were coming down. Friday morning we were unloading for a huge event." Doria, like Uhlir, was about to leave the Chicago Park District after working for the city in one capacity or another for more than twenty years when she was persuaded to help with the opening of Millennium Park by her former boss, Lois Weisberg, director of the Department of Cultural Affairs. All the focus had been on finishing the park; no one had thought seriously about what would go on inside it when it opened. With just four and a half months to go, Doria began work on the opening weekend. Bank One and J. P. Morgan Chase were underwriters for the $700,000 weekend event. Doria stayed on for several years, raising the roughly $3 million needed annually to cover the costs for the free programming in the park.

Doria's condition for accepting the job was that the park be kept under the authority of Weisberg and Cultural Affairs. Doria—who counts herself among Weisberg's numerous protégés—was depending on her old boss's political clout and protection. "Lois—people don't mess with her," Doria said. That's because Weisberg has a close relationship with the mayor and seems to have his confidence in a way that few others do. In her eighties by 2010, Weisberg has been director of Cultural Affairs since 1989. Doria's programming at Millennium Park is very much in the Weisberg tradition. Keeping the offerings free and varied exposes the greatest number of people to the arts and develops in them an appetite for more.

Enthusiasm in the audience is more important than distinctions between high, middle, and low art. "Because it's free," Doria said, "parents take advantage of introducing kids to things they wouldn't buy tickets for. At classical music programs, parents with kids sit at the back of the lawn so the kids can run around without disturbing anyone."

Even as plans for the opening proceeded, the Crown Fountain team was frantically refining technical issues to project the faces displayed on the Crown Fountain's glass towers. That work proceeded up until the last possible moment before the opening. A plan to have the mayor switch on the fountain's tower displays was judged too risky; better to keep the displays up and running than to chance the new system's failure at such a moment. The *Chicago Sun-Times* estimated that ten thousand people turned out for opening night. The mayor officially opened the park, together with John Bryan. "It's a people's park; it's for the people of Chicago," Daley said. Privately, he exulted over the success of the park and a victory over the "naysayers" who had criticized the park throughout its construction. The mayor was not the only one to feel that way. Uhlir was happy too. Harrowing weeks when the sound system at the Pritzker Pavilion had been challenged, tested, evaluated, and reevaluated had ended in success. Bryan predicted that people would come from all over the world to see Chicago's new park, just as they had traveled to Bilbao, Spain, to see Frank Gehry's Guggenheim Museum.

At 7:30 P.M., Cindy Pritzker greeted the crowd gathered at the pavilion named for her recently deceased husband, Jay, and toward which her family had donated $15 million. "Isn't this the spiffiest thing you ever saw?" she asked. It was unclear whether she was referring to the pavilion or the park. In any case, the people shouted their approval. The seventy-two-year-old Grant Park Orchestra and Chorus—the only remaining free, municipally funded orchestra in the country—finally had its own performance center. The program that night was conducted by music director Carlos Kalmar and included a piece, *Midsummer Fanfare,* commissioned for the occasion from composer John Corigliano.

The party continued through Saturday and Sunday. The park was crowded but not packed. The sound of laughing and shouting came from the Crown Fountain, where children had quickly figured out where to stand and when in order to take the full soaking brunt of the timed waterspout and waterfall. Jaume Plensa, the Spanish artist who designed the Crown Fountain and had taken an office in Chicago to monitor construction of his piece, said he was astonished and touched by the way his piece was embraced by the city. In the afternoons, everybody from African drummers to stilt walkers performed throughout the park. On top of the Harris Theater, pop music was performed, and Ira Glass of *This American*

Life told stories. People took their time walking across the BP Bridge, finding it the perfect vantage point from which to admire the park.

The last steel plate for *Cloud Gate* had arrived from the fabricator in California less than two weeks before opening day. It was in place, and although the sculpture was not finished, its form was complete. People loved it: they approached it, touched it, walked underneath it, and looked up into the belly button–like omphalos trying to locate their reflections.

They took pictures. The artist, Anish Kapoor, had fretted and argued when it was decided not to install his piece on Madison Street in the Lurie Garden but rather on the AT&T Plaza facing Michigan Avenue. But he loved the new location, where "it draws in the whole city so that this skyline is a part of the object." Closing the seams between the plates and polishing the steel to a near mirror finish would take almost two years more and would cost millions more. The sculpture was finished and rededicated on May 15, 2006.

The perennials for the Lurie Garden had been planted one month before the opening by Piet Oudolf, who had flown in from his native Holland to oversee the work himself. With years to go before the garden matured, visitors at the opening were puzzled by the great metal armature, taking it for a cage of some kind. "Are the trees trying to escape?" one person asked. (It would serve as a cutting guide when the hedge filled out.) "Louis the XIV had to wait for his garden too," landscape designer Kathryn Gustafson said tartly. It was hot, so children sat on the wooden deck and put their feet in the constructed limestone-bed stream that runs through the garden.

The negative press took a toll. The turnout for the three-day opening festivities was three hundred thousand, which sounds not bad until that number is compared to the Taste of Chicago, which in 2006 pulled in the same number on its first *day*. But if Millennium Park seemed to catch people off guard when it opened, they quickly realized that it belonged to them and there was no place like it. Nothing they had read or heard about the park had prepared them for it, and they have since embraced it ever more tightly and in ever growing numbers. In 2009, the park attracted four million visitors, taking its rightful place among Chicago's architectural and artistic wonders.

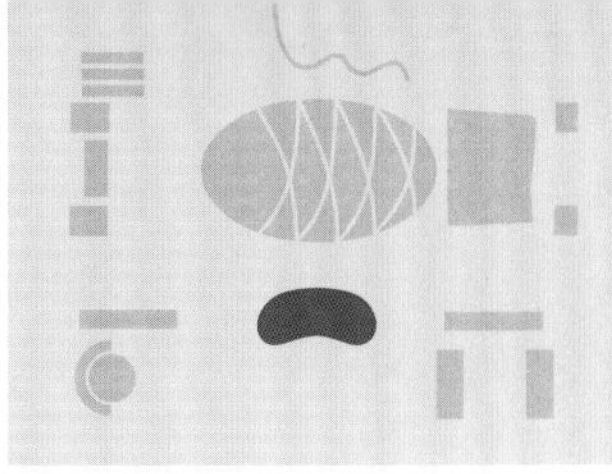

Cloud Gate

In order to get to the unreal, there's a lot of reality. There is weight, engineering, and the resolute pursuit of form and not letting go, not compromising whatever the result.

—ANISH KAPOOR

It looks weightless, improbable, and completely fascinating, like that perfect blob of mercury that rolled around on the bathroom floor after the old-fashioned glass thermometer broke, except that it is huge. It is 66 feet wide and 33 feet high, and it weighs 110 tons. The surface is a nearly perfect mirror that seems to slip back and forth between its own color—silver—and what it is reflecting: the blue of the sky, the buildings along Michigan Avenue, the people standing near it. It seems to appear and disappear while you look at it. Invariably, people also touch it as if to verify that the object really is present. The perfect surface reveals no clue as to how it was made. It is mysterious and beautiful. The name *Cloud Gate* seems fitting. The sculpture evokes the soft roundness and intangibility of a cloud, and the way it pulls the sky down to earth by reflecting its blueness does seem to offer an entryway to another realm.

This great, subtle sculpture had everyone fooled—except the artist who conceived it, Anish Kapoor—with its look of unassuming simplicity. Kapoor said he knew it would be difficult, and he thought it could be costly. In fact, it took heroic efforts by dozens of people and nearly $20 million in private money donated by corporations and individuals to achieve that appearance of perfect ease and weightlessness. Never has building the ephemeral been so arduous.

But, if ever there was a case to be made for the advantages of not knowing what you're getting into, *Cloud Gate* is it. Roark Frankel, an urban planner by training who supervised aspects of *Cloud Gate*'s construction for project manager US Equities, said, "If everyone had known what it would take, I don't think they would have done it." Shaking his head, he continues, "For it to get squashed for money or time, then I'm almost glad it got done this way. Look what it's going to bring to the city."

Public art and the artist

Until he was commissioned to create *Cloud Gate,* Anish Kapoor was ambivalent about contemporary public sculpture. This is his first permanent outdoor piece. Triumphal arches, generals on rearing stallions, memorials to soldiers—monuments such as these are shorthand for thoughts and feelings on which everyone agrees, whether it is pride, glory, or sorrow. Traditional public sculpture is a symbol and summary of society's judgment. We know how to read it. When there is no such agreement, the experience is jarring.

Kapoor's sculpture is abstract and open to interpretation, so he wondered what his work would communicate. In a country like the United States, where heterogeneity is the norm, what would we see when looking at his work? "It is not enough to have a little jewel on the lawn," he said. "For a public space to be meaningful, it has to lead the viewer beyond what is expected." Beauty is not enough, nor is it enough if only a few—the cognoscenti—"get" it. "I believe in the making of art, the viewer is all important," Kapoor said. What he realized he could do with *Cloud Gate* was "create a moment of reverie, a moment of dreaming." One could add, a moment of awe and wonder as well.

When the realization came to him that this public eloquence was within his powers, Kapoor also realized the expression would be an extension of work he had been doing for some time. His 1995 work *Turning the World Inside Out* is a stainless steel sphere, smaller in scale but conceptually related to *Cloud Gate,* as is a series of large, polished, stainless steel concave disks Kapoor created in the late 1990s. These pieces reflect and distort as *Cloud Gate* does. (The concave pieces also invert their reflections.) Paul Gray, of the Richard Gray Gallery, said, "A large part of the magic of Kapoor's work is the way it absorbs light and imagery . . . the reflective pieces absorb the environment around them."

Jeremy Strick, director of the Nasher Sculpture Center, recommended Kapoor for the park commission in 1999, when Strick was curator of twentieth-century art at the Art Institute of Chicago. Strick served on the Art Committee for the park and had been asked by John Bryan to name an artist for large public sculptures. Strick knew from experience that Kapoor's sculpture would work in a public setting. He recalls standing in line outside a gallery for a half hour "on a very rainy London day" to get inside to see the artist's work, and then "being completely, deeply engaged." Of Kapoor's work, Strick said, "It's abstract and spare, but it's also work people respond to; it captivates people. It has a connective power one doesn't always find in abstract work."

A visitor to the sculpture on a beautiful, late-August evening put it another way. "Human beings sure do like shiny objects," he said, surveying the crowd. A woman standing beside her friend inquired laughingly, "Where are you?" as she scanned the sculpture looking for her companion's reflection (the complex curves of the sculpture reflect indirectly, moving images to unexpected places). "There you are," she said upon finding her friend, and she took her picture. There were fingerprints everywhere on the sculpture that evening, going up as high as a person could reach.

How it could work

After Kapoor won the commission, he asked Lord Norman Foster of London, one of the world's most structurally venturesome architects, for advice on how to build it. "We had to find out how it was possible to make a single skin . . . no joints, no expansion joints, nothing of the kind. A single skin. How is it possible?" asked Kapoor. Foster told Kapoor that what he wanted to do was impossible. "Well," Kapoor said exultantly, "we found a way!"

An innovative British engineer Kapoor had worked with before, Christopher Hornzee-Jones, contributed a key structural concept, the precise structural analysis, and the plan to hold the steel plates that created the sculpture's rudimentary form in place until they could be welded together to make a completely integrated form in which the steel skin of the sculpture was also its structure, the thing that held it together. Hornzee-Jones devised a system that was as simple and pure as the sculpture's concept.

Everything in *Cloud Gate* is structural, and everything is made of stainless steel. The engineer took into account Chicago's immoderate temperatures, which can vary 100 degrees or more over the course of a year. Using one material was the only way to be certain the natural expansion and contraction that occur over the seasons would be uniform throughout the sculpture. With complete material integrity, *Cloud Gate* would suffer no broken seams or joints caused by differential expansion and contraction.

Cloud Gate looks as though it has been frozen in mid-bounce. That weightless appearance comes partly from the way the sculpture meets the ground in just two small places. It has an internal armature formed of large, single rings placed inside at opposite ends of the sculpture and connected to one another by a truss running the width of the sculpture. The rings transfer the weight of the sculpture down to two points connected to a massive wall beneath the park that supports *Cloud Gate*'s 110 tons.

What gives mercury its weird, self-contained property is high surface tension; in other words, even though it is liquid, it holds itself together. So it is with *Cloud Gate*. There were 168 steel plates of one-quarter- to three-sixteenths-inch thickness. Each plate weighed roughly two thousand pounds. In a laborious process, the plates were put in place and held there by a series of cables and springs until all of them could be invisibly attached to one another with structural welds. After the welding was finished, the springs and cables were removed. When the curtain is lifted on something that looks simple, there are usually tricks, but there are no tricks here. *Cloud Gate* is both form and structure. What you see is what you get.

Making it

It would be left to Ethan Silva, sole proprietor of Performance Structures in Oakland, California, to find a way to make *Cloud Gate.* Silva has been in the business of fabricating exotic structures for more than twenty-five years, having built sets for touring rock bands including U2, the Rolling Stones, and Pink Floyd, and at least one ride for an amusement park. In his late fifties by 2010, he is an arrogant, blunt, combative, and tenacious man. He does not mind making people angry. If he wins their respect in the meantime, that's fine, and if he doesn't, that's fine too. In the end, only one opinion of his work mattered to him, and that was Kapoor's. Silva's background (studies in science and fine art and an early career as a boat builder) is unusual but was weirdly, if not perfectly, suited to solving *Cloud Gate*'s challenges. Silva had even built a huge mechanical "mirror ball" that opened and closed during a Pink Floyd show. Still, Silva said of the first time he saw drawings of *Cloud Gate,* "I knew it was trouble." But he was captivated by the concept.

His first thought was to circumvent the really tough structural problems by making the form out of concrete and then covering it with molten metal. That would be easier than the skin the artist imagined, and it would achieve the seamless finish the artist wanted.

John Bryan had no interest in compromise solutions. He said no to Silva's idea; it had to be a steel skin structure. In the original project description, the Art Committee asked for a sculpture that would stand for one thousand years. Bryan took that brief seriously. Similarly, when Kapoor was asked to reduce the size of *Cloud Gate,* it was Bryan who rejected the suggestion.

Silva said he does not take on a project if it was engineered without his involvement, so he was there as Hornzee-Jones and other engineers, some brought to the table by Silva, solved *Cloud Gate*'s structural and assembly problems. Although it would be challenging, Silva believed that what they devised could be built. "We designed it like a boat," he said.

The fundamental challenge of *Cloud Gate* was to make an exquisitely refined piece of art using fairly crude industrial techniques and materials. Kapoor wanted the level of craftwork one would expect to find in a finely made piece of gold or platinum jewelry, but he wanted the piece made out of stainless steel on a colossal, unprecedented scale.

Silva came up with a process that combined old technology with new and exacting methods of measurement. An industrial tool called the English wheel shaped the flat plates to prescribed curves by applying tremendous regulated force in a continuous rolling, circular motion. During this process, the plates are more or less shoved through the machine by a crew of as many as three. The shaped plates were digitally scanned and measured by a robotic device called a FaroArm to see if they matched the sculpture's computerized model. When a panel did not match precisely, it went back on the wheel. Bending the steel creates material tension. To stabilize the plates, each of them was baked at a high temperature in an oven custom-built for the purpose by Silva's company. A shaped, high-relief steel grid welded to

the back of each plate added strength and would provide the necessary attachment points for assembling the sculpture.

The work was laborious and intense, but the process was working. The sculpture was being assembled in Silva's enormous company studio; the internal ring frame was up, and the plates were being put in place as they were shaped. The level of precision being achieved was extraordinary. The team was aiming for a tolerance between adjacent plates equal to the width of three human hairs; in many cases they were achieving the width of one.

It was, however, all taking much longer than Silva had expected. Fabrication and assembly were only part of it. There was finishing work to do as well—the precision welding that would eliminate those hairline openings between the plates and then polishing *Cloud Gate* to a mirror finish. Said Frankel, "[Silva's] a genius, but he had never done this before. He wasn't unaware of the complexity. He had lots of confidence in his ability, but he did not know how he would do it. He was uncovering and solving problems as he went." Silva had said it would take two years; in the end it would take a little over three.

The plan was to do all the work at Silva's warehouse and studio on the Oakland waterfront. Then the sculpture was to begin a forty-five-day journey, moving by oceangoing vessel going south, transiting the Panama Canal, and then heading back north and cutting inland through the St. Lawrence Seaway and eventually onto Lake Michigan, where it was to be disembarked at Queen's Landing opposite Buckingham Fountain. Frankel and others at US Equities had even developed plans to dredge the harbor if the water level was too low to accommodate the ship. From there, by Frankel's calculations, it would have taken two to three days to bring *Cloud Gate* on a series of dollies forming a single trailer with 128 wheels coordinated by networked microcomputers to inch the sculpture over the Monroe Bridge—itself shored up to take the sculpture's weight—to its site at Millennium Park. Frankel still regrets that the spectacle never took place.

By October 3, 2003, with about one-third of the sculpture completed and assembled in California, it was clear that *Cloud Gate* would not be finished and in place for the Millennium Park opening if the plans did not change. If it had been halfway finished, Frankel says, "There would still have been a chance [Silva] would have made it in time." As it was, US Equities directed Silva to dismantle what he had and ship it to Chicago by truck. The succeeding plates would be sent by truck also as they were finished in California. *Cloud Gate* would be built in Chicago, not California.

With piecemeal overland shipping, on-site assembly, and finishing, costs for *Cloud Gate* would increase again, and substantially. In August 2002, Silva told the Chicago team his

RENTAL | SHOP | RESTROOMS
PARK GRILL
GRILL | CAFE | PARKING
PARK CAFE
SKATE
EAT
PLAY

original pricing for the project was so far off that he would be bankrupted if he continued under the terms of his original contract. He threatened to quit work on the sculpture and won an agreement based on a time-and-materials basis with no further profit for his company.

There was no alternative to constructing it in Chicago if *Cloud Gate* were to be in place for the park opening. The assembly crew would at least gain the forty-five days that shipping the fully formed piece would have taken. In addition, delay on the sculpture would have meant delays elsewhere. The Chase Promenade could not be constructed until the sculpture was in place because the promenade was the route along which the sculpture was to be brought into the park. If the sculpture were built on its site, promenade construction could proceed.

MTH Industries was hired to assemble *Cloud Gate* in Chicago. The six members from Ironworkers Local 63 who started the job remained on the project throughout as the crew grew to as many as twenty-six. Nick Taylor, himself an artist and sculptor, arrived from California to help coordinate the work and train and supervise the crew. Taylor had worked with Silva on several projects over the years and would prove to be a strong on-site advocate for maintaining exacting standards in finishing and polishing *Cloud Gate*.

Two generators and two air compressors were moved to the site to power handheld tools. Beginning in February 2004, the workers quickly rebuilt what Silva had completed. The sculpture was being built from the bottom up. The finished steel plates, each one carried in a custom-made crate, began to arrive every week. The plates were tack-welded in place; final structural welding would be done when the form was complete. As the sculpture went up, the tight tolerances made fitting the pieces together increasingly challenging. On July 3, 2004, with Millennium Park's opening date just days away, the last plate arrived and was eased into place.

Opening day

"That's the star of the show," Frank Gehry said of *Cloud Gate*. The city greeted *Cloud Gate* with an appreciation matching Gehry's. Most people did not even realize the sculpture was unfinished. It looked nearly immaculate. The only evidence of its unfinished state was the thin lines between the plates that made up the sculpture and the tiny dots where tack welds held the plates to the temporary inner cables. Even imperfect, it was beautiful.

Kapoor, in Chicago for the park's opening, praised the work done to fabricate his sculpture at a symposium at the Art Institute on July 23, 2004. He described what the additional work on *Cloud Gate* would produce. "I'm interested in a condition of perfection. . . . The very subtle thing that I've been trying to get to is when you make an object to a level of perfection that is beyond the hand, beyond it being made, something happens. . . . It turns into a kind of nonobject. It's that condition I'm looking for. . . . One ought not to be able to tell what the form is. For now, you can see it is in its incomplete state. It's much more of an object than I'd like it to be. I'm looking for that unreality which I think and hope will come."

Frankel, recalling the warmth of *Cloud Gate*'s initial reception, said he was elated by what had been accomplished and deeply worried about the next step. "The detailing wasn't there. To get it how it should be, we had to leave the safe harbor of what we had. We had to take this thing that everyone loved, this beautiful thing, and make it look worse to make it better. It was scary. The process [of completing the welding and making the hairline cracks disappear] would turn it black and [temporarily] deform it. To willingly make it ugly . . ." Frankel's voice trailed off before he continued, "We tested, but we could never fully mock up the conditions. What if you spent all the extra time and money and it wasn't better?" A few, including some at US Equities, which had been publicly criticized for its management of the job, argued for leaving well enough alone. Kapoor was adamant that the work proceed. Silva agreed.

Finishing

In January 2005, *Cloud Gate* disappeared under a tent so structural welding could begin. This process would seal the hairline openings between plates and make *Cloud Gate* self-contained and self-supporting, "a single skin," in Kapoor's phrase.

In the summer of 2005, with ten days still to go before *Cloud Gate* was to be unveiled for the second time with all but a fraction of its skin polished to a near mirror finish, Chicago had staggered through more than thirty days of ninety-degree-plus weather. For ten more days, the steelworkers would work in an enclosed, non-air-conditioned tent where, until they got rid of it, the thermometer would hit 125 degrees more than once. The crew of twenty-two was working twelve-hour days, five days per week.

Perfect structural welds (also called full-penetration welds) are usually for industrial applications, so they do not have to be undetectable. Who cares if a tank's seams are smooth? For *Cloud Gate,* the welds had to be perfect and undetectable. The crew members were embarking on new territory when they began this stage. They knew the parameters. The steel could not be overheated because it would be irreversibly discolored, so welds were made at temperatures of seven hundred to nine hundred degrees rather than the usual twenty-four hundred. The welds had to be slightly elevated so that there would be something to grind away when polishing began. To do that, every seam was manually clamped from inside the sculpture to push the plate edges out very slightly—just one thirty-second of an inch—before welding. Indenting the surface, no matter how slightly, meant a "wow," the term the crew used to describe a dimple that would magnify as many as five thousand times an imperfect, wavering reflection on *Cloud Gate*'s surface. The welding proceeded with two crews of four: one team inside the sculpture doing the clamping; the other, outside, operating the torches.

The team planned on polishing about 2,400 linear feet. That would have covered the welded seams and a few inches on either side. But the welding had caused deformation over larger areas than expected. The polishing required went up to 9,600 linear feet, with six inches to be polished on either side of the seam. Despite the enormous increase in the scope of the polishing, the crew had another fixed deadline to meet. They had to be finished by August 28, 2005, when *Cloud Gate* was scheduled for its second unveiling.

Aside from scorching summer heat, the workers faced other hardships. It was difficult to get to the high and the low areas of the sculpture. Scaffolding could not touch the sculpture because it would mar the surface, so workers were suspended in harnesses like the ones window washers use in order to reach and finish the topmost sections. They lay on their backs to reach the bottom sections, holding above their heads tools that weighed up to eighteen pounds.

The conventional tools for polishing steel were modified specifically for *Cloud Gate.* One type of sander was fitted with outrigger feet that helped prevent grinding too deep. The crew worked the same areas over again and again, sometimes spending as much as two days getting one seam polished correctly. Taylor was the one who inspected and said when an area was finished. Polishing ten linear feet ate up between seventy-five and one hundred sanding belts. At the edge of the tent, there were hundreds and hundreds of dusty black garbage bags containing spent belts waiting to be carried away.

In the course of the project, these steelworkers became artisans, a crew possessed of gifts so rare and refined that they may never have call to use them again. They were dedicated to the work, knowing they were helping to make something exceptional. At one point, the entire crew, including Taylor, threatened to walk off the job if they were not permitted to finish the polishing to a higher level of quality.

Kapoor said, "It's better-made than anything I've ever made." Of the workers, he said, "There is a tremendous sense of communal effort. It's heroic, absolutely heroic what they have done." Silva tells of one worker, Rick Brown, who brought his son, Tommy, to see *Cloud Gate.* Brown brought the child inside the sculpture and let him sign his name on one of the steel plates, saying the boy would always be proud to know his father helped build *Cloud Gate.*

The unveiling

When *Cloud Gate* was unveiled on August 28, 2005, it had acquired that slippery, unreal quality Kapoor was after. About the sculpture's reception, Kapoor said, "That is the most wonderful thing I know of. I can calculate for scale, I cannot calculate for what people will feel." Even so, the power of the piece surprises even the artist. "I could never quite have imagined the vista, the way it brings in the city. I knew it would collect the city and sky. . . . This mysterious globule fits in because it brings in everything else."

Having seen *Cloud Gate,* the way it works outdoors and among people—"Fingerprints are very much OK," said Kapoor—it is difficult to think of Kapoor's work contained in an interior anymore. This enormous mirror, intent on absorbing everything, would go hungry in a mere room.

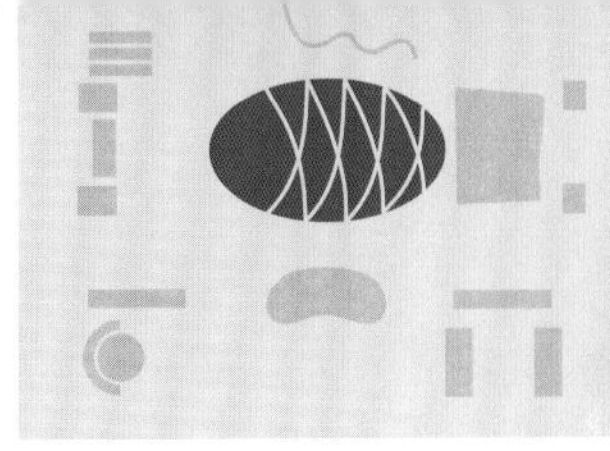

Jay Pritzker Pavilion

If we had somebody like Frank Gehry, that would be *the art.*
—CINDY PRITZKER

Approach Millennium Park from Washington Street. That is far better than the oblique walk along Michigan Avenue, where the park can be glimpsed, anticipated, guessed at, and prepared for as you draw closer. It is best to see it head-on in the summary view framed at the east end of Washington. There, with only the sky as backdrop and light reflecting off it, is an enormous billowing steel sail, looking as though it were filled by a stiff wind from the north, blowing across the space between nineteenth-century buildings. This is the profile view of the Jay Pritzker Pavilion, and from this crowded urban context, the sight is fully astonishing. More than mere juxtaposition, this angle captures the unlikely context within which the pavilion arose. But there it is, the hardworking, dense, orthogonal downtown that created an open-sky, modern-day celebration.

"This ain't a puny thing," Frank Gehry said in an interview as he described his just-unveiled design for the Pritzker Pavilion. Indeed. At 120 feet, the pavilion is roughly as tall as a twelve-story building. The performance hall, an open wooden box, is framed by curling stainless steel ribbons that pantomime, in exclamatory fashion, music's diffusive quality. The arcing trellis lightly covering the elliptical lawn where the audience sits offers a complementary sense of embrace. When Gehry, after some prodding, agreed to take the commission, he described what he wanted to do. "I'd like to design the relationship between the audience and the stage, because that's a magical thing when it works."

Ed Uhlir said yes to that. But Gehry's ambition for the project, as he described it, is revealing. From the start, he saw his task as using architecture to support something intangible, creating a "relationship" that would enhance the spectators' experience. Architecture would be the foil for the performance. He did not emulate the pure white gallery cube that takes nothing away from the art on the wall (although he briefly explored a scheme in that spirit). Rather than the architecture disappearing in deference to performance, Gehry's design is flamboyant and assertive. The result: the architecture resonates like a tuning fork at the same exhibitionist pitch as performance itself, creating harmony between the set and the staged. Sculpture, spectacle, stage set, and functionally refined building—the Pritzker Pavilion is all of these things.

The start

The Pritzker Pavilion is also the beginning of Millennium Park as we know it now. Before Gehry was engaged, the master plan designed by Skidmore, Owings & Merrill (SOM) called for a classical Beaux Arts park similar in style to Grant Park to be built on top of a constructed deck covering railway lines and a parking garage. As a plan to make a park out of thin air in the very heart of one of America's largest, densest cities, it was bold, but aesthetically, the scheme was conservative.

Cindy Pritzker, a member of the Millennium Park Arts Committee, was unhappy. Describing the planners, she said, "I don't think they were in the twentieth century. Really, they were doing old Chicago." She told John Bryan, the committee chair, "If we had somebody like Frank Gehry, that would *be* the art." As cofounder with her husband, Jay, of the prestigious Pritzker Architecture Prize, which was awarded to Gehry in 1989, Cindy Pritzker had both a warm friendship with the architect and a certain authority on the matter of architectural merit. She thought, "It's going to be today and tomorrow, not yesterday." Edward Uhlir and James Feldstein were dispatched to Gehry's office in California in December 1998 to ask him to design the pavilion. Gehry and Pritzker said they did not talk to one another about the project before Uhlir arrived. Gehry's first response was negative. The project was not big enough, Gehry said. It was too far away. He had no time for it. Then, finally, Uhlir played his ace, saying, "Cindy will be disappointed." And Gehry said, "OK, I'll do it."

He had taken the job, but the fact remained that he had no time. "It was humanly impossible to do it in time for the millennium," he said. He could not even begin working on

the design for six months because of existing projects. Uhlir agreed to wait; getting Gehry was more important than the millennium deadline.

Gehry's initial "no" came partly from misunderstanding the offer. He had been contacted earlier about the pavilion and asked to collaborate on it with the then design architect, SOM. Gehry understood this overture as an invitation to adorn somebody else's building with his once trademark fish motif, and he turned it down. "I don't do fish sculptures," he said later. (He might have added "anymore," since he had done large fish sculptures for an exhibition of his work at the Walker Art Center in Minneapolis in 1986 that traveled to the Whitney Museum of Art in New York and—in collaboration with SOM and design architect Bruce Graham in 1992—designed a fish for the roof of the Vila Olímpica hotel in Barcelona that is nothing if not sculpture.) Gehry believed Uhlir was coming to see him with some version of the earlier proposal, not to design the entire pavilion. "So then I understood the whole thing," Gehry said.

Having agreed to the pavilion, Gehry asked, "What's that?" He was pointing at the park plan where the pedestrian bridge was to go. "I've never done a bridge before," he said. Before the meeting with Uhlir and Feldstein ended, Gehry had the pavilion and the BP Bridge to design too.

Hiring Gehry was the beginning of Millennium Park's evolution from a traditional park to what it is now, a radically new urban gathering place. Not incidentally, it was this ratcheting up of ambitions for Millennium Park, first signaled by the pavilion, that slowed the park's completion, made it more costly, and, ultimately, made it extraordinary.

"With Gehry in there, that raised the bar," Cindy Pritzker said. "People became excited about it." She meant that both donors, like herself, and artists who might install work there were zeroing in on the park. The Pritzker family donated $15 million for constructing the pavilion. The City of Chicago's figures put the total cost for the pavilion at $50 million. Some critics of the park say it was substantially more. "We decided we needed to do something," said Cindy Pritzker. “We stepped up fast, and we thought it would get others excited.” With Jay suffering the effects of a stroke, Cindy discussed the donation with their son, Tom Pritzker, first. But the entire family, including Jay’s brother, Robert Pritzker, approved the gift. “We did it as a family,” Cindy explained. Jay Pritzker died January 23, 1999, without seeing the pavilion that bears his name completed.

The design

Before Frank Gehry did museums, he did music halls. There is the Walt Disney Concert Hall in Los Angeles (1987–2003), where Gehry married his mature, animated architectural style to his deep knowledge about performance spaces. (Construction of the Disney hall was delayed for years because the design was controversial and hard to build.) But early in his career, Gehry designed two outdoor music pavilions in a rather conservative design style. One is in Maryland, and the other is in California; both stand in formed earthen bowls that help the acoustics.

The project Gehry points to, however, as teaching him about music, audiences, and architecture is the Hollywood Bowl in Hollywood, California, which Gehry did not design but reworked and reworked again between 1972 and 1982 to improve it acoustically and to give it more architectural presence. With an acoustic engineer, Gehry devised an inexpensive, impermanent solution. Using sixty twenty-foot-tall cardboard tubes suspended above

Prudential

and standing on end around the stage, the architect made a crudely effective sound system. In place, the tubes looked like a tongue-in-cheek, classical colonnade. In 1980, Gehry's permanent design for the Hollywood Bowl—large, variously sized, fiberglass globes mounted inside the shell's arc and projecting past the edge of the band shell—was installed and augmented with new sound technology. The bowl does not look like the Pritzker Pavilion but influenced it. The sound-deflection principle is essentially the same. Also similar is the way Gehry pulled audience and architecture together by projecting functional acoustic pieces out over the seats. "That hood that comes out over the [Pritzker Pavilion] stage does reflect sound down to the seats. The ones on the side do act to contain the sound in the space where the audience is. So, 75 percent of all that stuff is pretty functional and rational," Gehry explained.

For the Pritzker Pavilion, Gehry ramped up the architectural scale and amplified what he had learned at the Hollywood Bowl. This is a democratic design, one that makes everybody a participant. It is the answer to the question Gehry posed to himself, "How to get an outdoor space where the people who are far away from the orchestra feel like they are included in the performance? [So they feel] that it was as special for them as it was for the people in the front seats?" From the back of the audience's lawn, the pavilion is as strong as it is up close. It is architecture that reaches out across space to grab people. Its power is such that most people lounging on the lawn when there is no performance still sit facing it, as though it had some magnetic force, rather than facing each other.

There are four thousand fixed seats and room for another seven thousand people on the lawn. "The shell itself is wood, because it's warm and beautiful," said Gehry. Lighted, it contrasts nicely with the steel wings surrounding the stage. Enormous, folding, custom-made glass doors measuring fifty by one hundred feet close the stage off from the elements when it is not in use. The stage is occasionally rented out as a hall for special events.

The trellis was also inspired by the audience. "All of it is about connecting the audience to the performer and the performer to the audience," said Gehry. Touching down only along the edge of the elliptically shaped field, where it is supported by columns, the trellis conjures a feeling of enclosure for the audience, blocking neither sight lines to the stage nor the view of the sky. Its principal function is to support lighting and the speakers that are placed every seventy feet and provide the distributed, equalized sound system for the audience. Nothing like it has ever before been built for an outdoor performance space. The design is direct and elegant, spare where the pavilion is baroque, subtle where the pavilion is thrillingly bombastic. The trellis stands down to let the pavilion step forward.

Arguably, between the pavilion and the trellis, the trellis is the more structurally daring. It has twenty-two arches with extremely long, unsupported spans, some of them more than four hundred feet. The basket weave where the arcs of the trellis intersect provides the additional strength and rigidity necessary to sustain the length. And Gehry, acting against type, made the trellis absolutely minimal architecturally. The steel tubes that make up the trellis are between twelve and twenty inches in diameter depending on their position. They are as big as they need to be to keep the structure aloft and no more.

At work

Gehry's serious work is done making models—many, many models. "I have models in my face all day long," he complained. Each one is used to try out a different form or a permutation on an earlier idea. The models are rarely neat; crumpled pieces of paper may stand in for chaotic effects, and Scotch tape often serves as mortar. He models at two different levels of scale, one with the project in isolation and one as it would appear in its context of surrounding structures and landscapes included. Working at both levels keeps him from becoming infatuated with form and forces him to think through and create an appropriate relationship between his project and its surroundings.

For the Pritzker Pavilion, Gehry estimates that he made twenty models. Early on, he considered a very simple design. He called this his "Miesian scheme" in honor of the famous German modernist architect Ludwig Mies van der Rohe, who made his home in Chicago and designed some of the city's most honored buildings. For that design, Gehry worked to get to the essence of the design problem by asking himself, "What is the least I can do?" The design that came out of that inquiry was uncharacteristically simple, geometric, and unadorned. At various times, Gehry has said this was a serious design solution and that it was nothing more than a preliminary scheme. But it seems likely that Chicago, with its splendid modernist architectural tradition, caused even Frank Gehry, who seems entitled at this point to being intimidation-proof, to think about restraint. In any case, he showed the design to Cindy Pritzker when she visited his office, and she let him know that it was not what she had in mind. "It didn't look like Frank, and I thought if we were going to do Frank, it should look like Frank," she explained. To Gehry, she said bluntly, "Frank, that looks like the Grant Park band shell." He went back to work, and then, as Pritzker said simply, "It happened." The design came together.

Designing for the neighborhood

Given his work, Gehry's professed concern for urban context may seem surprising. How does a Gehry building, with its curves and strange materials, relate to conventional structures with their corners, straight lines, and bricks, wood, and stone? How can Gehry see his work as anything other than scene stealing?

But Gehry is sensitive to the way buildings and cities interact. After completing his undergraduate architecture degree at the University of Southern California in 1954, he studied urban planning at the graduate school at Harvard University. And in 1960 he worked for André Remondet's firm in Paris, where he absorbed the lessons in urbanism offered on the streets of one of the world's most graceful cities. Unlike most people, Gehry does not think of the relationships among buildings and cities just in terms of similarity. He expands the idea of interaction sometimes by contradiction, sometimes by exaggeration, and only sometimes by affinity. In Prague, he designed a pair of office buildings nicknamed "Ginger and Fred" (1996, properly known as the Nationale-Nederlanden Building), because one of the structures is curved into the other like a dancer leaning into her partner, evocative of the silver screen's famous hoofers Ginger Rogers and Fred Astaire. The curved building stands on a corner overlooking the Vltava River and a public square. The building's bend acknowledges the important location with a curtsy and emphasizes the importance of the city corner as an opening, a recurring rhythmic beat in the urban tempo.

Rather than a grandstander, Gehry is known as a collaborator, albeit an unorthodox one. He understands collaboration in the same way he understands interaction: it is not quiet, it is not about mimicking, it is about challenge. The Guggenheim in Bilbao (1997) was designed with the installation of Richard Serra's work in mind; rarely has architecture accommodated art more harmoniously. At Vila Olímpica, Gehry's partner in design was Bruce Graham of SOM, who died in 2010 but in his lifetime was as famous in architecture circles for his colossal ego and titanic temper as he was for the design of the Hancock Building, the Sears (now Willis) Tower, and the Inland Steel Building. When Gehry heard that Renzo Piano would design a bridge from his addition to the Art Institute of Chicago to Millennium Park, he interpreted it as a challenge from an architect of enormous stature. "I told him to come after me," Gehry said.

Describing the pavilion before it was built, Gehry said it would be like "a bouquet of flowers on the table." Just like the Guggenheim in Bilbao, Spain, it is an urban centerpiece. Although fully intended as spectacles, these buildings are not alien to their environments. To see one design connection, return to Washington Street at Wabash and wait for the silver elevated train to streak through your view of the Pritzker Pavilion. What you see at that

instant is emblematic Chicago and pure motion juxtaposed in front of Gehry's steel, abstract sculpture of the same.

Gehry says often that he has a special respect and affection for Chicago. He visited the city as a boy with his father, a salesman, on a rare weeklong trip the two took together. They stayed at a YMCA. The impression the city made on him as a child is tinged by warm recollections of his father, who was often away from home because of his work. "It was one of the few times I spent with him like that," Gehry said. In the 1950s, Gehry returned as a student of architecture to look at Frank Lloyd Wright's work. Clearly, Gehry took to heart Wright's famous command to "break out of the box." More recently, Gehry has said Chicago is the North American city most like Paris in its "body language." Chicago's relationship to Lake Michigan and the city's contrasting dense mass of architecture make it, he said, "probably the best American city." In 2005, Gehry helped put together the purchase of—and became a small stakeholder in—a landmark of Chicago architecture, Graham's Inland Steel Building, now named for its address, 30 West Monroe (SOM, 1957). That building's novel stainless steel cladding, Gehry said, influenced his own work.

How to build it

Aside from scale, there is not much difference between Gehry's final model and the building in Millennium Park today. Given the design's complexity, this is a large achievement. To start, the pavilion stands on top of another building, a parking garage that was not initially designed to support anything more than its own weight. The garage had to be reinforced. Then there is the pavilion itself. Steel beams stretch out unsupported as far as 120 feet from the proscenium; the shortest is 78 feet. At the far end of those long cantilevers are the heaviest elements, the steel ribbons, which, with their curling shapes, are devilishly vulnerable to winds and to winter's additional burden of snow and ice. Engineering the thing was not easy.

"Frank Gehry is very particular. These are not designed just willy-nilly. He wants what is built to be very close to what he designed," said John Zils, the pavilion's lead structural engineer. It was largely Zils's responsibility to make the pavilion work as the architect imagined. The Pritzker is the third project, after the Guggenheim at Bilbao and Vila Olímpica in Barcelona, that Zils engineered in collaboration with Gehry. Zils has worked his entire forty-year career at SOM (the firm was retained for engineering the pavilion). For the first sixteen years at SOM, Zils worked under the man who hired him straight out of school, Fazlur Kahn, the brilliant engineer for Chicago's sky-busting Hancock Building and Sears Tower.

So Zils is unfazed by challenging designs. But as an engineer who cut his teeth on the foursquare modernist buildings that distinguished SOM in the 1950s, '60s, and '70s, how does he adjust to Gehry's curvaceous work? "It's a 180-degree shift" from the work he does customarily, Zils said. Describing Gehry's designs, Zils said, "They are free-form, but they are not arbitrary. Gehry is very interested in how we can provide a structure with some economy in it. . . . This is not a case of 'Here it is, make it work.'"

Just as Gehry did, Zils looked for the essence of the problem. "I try to find some mechanism to simplify and rationalize the problem," Zils said. He imagined a three-dimensional structural grid with ten-foot by nine-foot, eight-inch square modules standing behind the curling steel elements. Why not just ten feet square? The grid's dimensions were driven in part by an interest in economy and the garage structure below, where the columns on one axis were placed every twenty-nine feet, a multiple of nine feet, eight inches. "Every third element would come down on existing structure," Zils said. Without this accommodation, a complicated and costly system for transferring the weight of the pavilion to supports elsewhere would have been necessary.

With the support grid's measurements defined, Zils's team dissected Gehry's design on a computer, slicing it vertically at nine-foot, eight-inch intervals and slicing it again horizontally at ten-foot intervals. Zils had his simple and rational tool, a structural system against which each point in every curve could be referenced and to which every piece of steel could be attached in construction.

Unlike the Guggenheim at Bilbao, where the interior and exterior forms correspond, the complex shapes at the Pritzker are essentially a false front forming a headdress atop the stage. Given that, Zils could employ another economy by avoiding the expense of fabricating a support system following every bend and curve. Instead, he used a more affordable system of straight support sections with angled attachment arms. Said Zils, "Even Gehry doesn't have an unlimited budget." There are 697 plates attached like shingles to form the headdress. The panels themselves are nearly fourteen inches thick and are made mostly of aluminum with a thin outer sheet of stainless steel only one thirty-second of an inch thick.

Placing the curved headdress panels was extremely difficult. The smallest deviation in installing one piece threw off the placement of succeeding plates in a cascading effect. The phenomenon of incremental differentiation meant that all 697 plates on the headdress had to be repositioned with the help of an extremely precise three-dimensional laser system after the first installment of the plates went wrong.

The design for the trellis evolved in a give-and-take process between architect and engineer. As it changed, it became more effective functionally and more beautiful.

Straight spans were considered first, but the angled, interwoven spans, although longer, made a lighter and more rigid structure possible. The basket-weave design also better complemented the pavilion's forms and the egg-shaped field. Gehry imagined each arc in the trellis as a double curve, bent along both the horizontal and vertical axes. The arcs would have been difficult to fabricate that way; holding the precise arc of the first curve while making the second bend is not easy. Zils suggested instead that the arcs be curved on one axis only and then rolled to the side when they were installed to create the appearance of a double curve. That solution worked and was both easier to accomplish and less expensive.

The most complex area to engineer and build was known on the building site as the X node. Located about eighty feet up in the air, it is the place where the two structures—the pavilion and the trellis—intersect and where the catwalk for lighting the stage is located. Everything comes together at that point, and there are not many right angles. "It was very difficult to visualize in three dimensions," said Zils. "You looked up and it looked like a Swiss watch when it was in construction."

During construction, shoring towers held the long cantilevers in place until they were fully loaded with the steel sails. In spring 2003, the towers were removed. Zils said, "That was a big day." He had expected some drop at the tip of the beams when the supports were taken away. Ready for a deflection of four inches, he was relieved to see it was just under that, at about three and a half.

Acoustics

In Ed Uhlir's retelling, Mayor Richard M. Daley phoned him after a bad night's sleep. The mayor woke up in the middle of the night with a question: "What if the acoustics don't work?" The combination of the trellis and the distributed sound system was unprecedented, and the mayor wanted reassurance. Uhlir brought in a series of acousticians, experts in an inexact science, to evaluate the system. They disagreed with one another. Uhlir brought in more experts. Deborah Borda, chief executive officer of the Los Angeles Philharmonic, told Uhlir, "You get three acousticians in the same room and ask them the same question; you'll get six different answers." After several weeks of testing and talking to consultants, the system passed the test, and the quality of sound at the pavilion has since been praised by many music critics.

How did he do that?

Gehry's buildings provoke awe even among people who may not like them. They beg an answer to the question, "How did he do that?" The Pritzker Pavilion, with its struts and buttresses exposed, shows how it is done. That is a unique feature in Gehry's recent work, and it is especially appropriate in Chicago, where the great, experimental architecture of Louis Sullivan, John Wellborn Root, Ludwig Mies van der Rohe, and Bertrand Goldberg, among others, has always celebrated structural honesty.

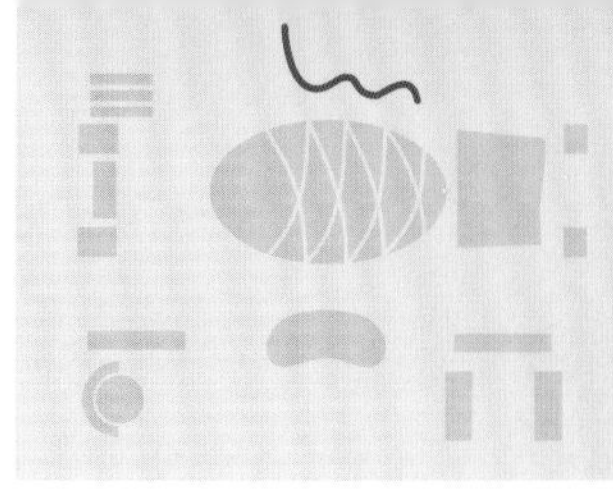

BP Bridge

The evolution of [my architectural] language really came from a desire to express movement and feeling through inert materials.

—FRANK GEHRY

This is not an ordinary bridge with ordinary bridge objectives. No straight charge between two points at the narrowest pass; this bridge meanders, curves, and bends. At 925 feet in length, it is an extended invitation to everyone to take their time. Spanning the four-lane Columbus Drive, the BP Bridge serves as a link connecting Millennium Park with part of Grant Park. But most people cross the BP Bridge to recross it. It is the passage that counts. So people stroll and roll across the bridge—with its gentle slope, it easily accommodates wheelchairs and baby strollers—and then go back the way they came, taking in one of the best views of Gehry's Pritzker Pavilion.

The bridge starts climbing obliquely from inside Millennium Park, rising parallel to the pavilion's Great Lawn before turning east to cross the road. This unorthodox bridge is clad with shingled steel plates enfolding the sides and underside of the bridge, creating hazy, continuously changing reflections. (Passing beneath the bridge in a car on Columbus Drive is another, different pleasure.) The waist-high walls are flat steel panels; the deck is a wood similar in hardness and durability to teak. "I insisted on it being wood because concrete would not have been as endearing to walk on," said Gehry. Approaching the bridge to cross back to the park from Daley Bicentennial Plaza, a new aspect presents itself. Now the approach is direct and frontal; the bridge's shingled sides curling back and up rise overhead like the high crests of waves seen from the bottom trough.

Fish stories

Gehry used to tell a story about his boyhood. Every Thursday, he would watch mesmerized when a doomed carp brought home from the market swam in the bathtub until his grandmother butchered it on Friday to make gefilte fish. "I played with it," he said. He told this story by way of explanation for fish imagery's totemlike status in his work. Gehry designed a building in Tokyo in the form of a leaping fish; he made lights that look like fish; he created museum installations that included rooms in the shape of fish that visitors inhabited like Jonah did the whale. Gehry's funny and oddly touching story has to do with the impossibility of achieving perfection. To this architect, fish are the ideal union of structure, form, and purpose, the epitome of all that great architecture aspires to be. But as living creatures that move and change continuously, fish are also much more than architecture can ever be. "The fish . . . started to become for me like a symbol for a certain kind of perfection that I couldn't achieve with my buildings," Gehry said.

Accepting the impossibility of duplicating the fish's fluid vitality in fixed structures, Gehry settles for emulation. That he sets movement or the illusion of movement as a goal for his work speaks volumes about his ambition as well as the challenges he poses to his profession. His ideal is contrary to the very essence of architecture throughout time, that is, stability. "The evolution of [my architectural] language really came from a desire to express movement and feeling through inert materials," Gehry said. Sometimes he gets very close. There is a moment looking from the west side of the bridge to the span crossing the road where the likeness is acute. The bridge's underside looks exactly like a fish caught in the act of turning in the water, its shingled cladding shining like scales.

The unique architectural challenge of bridges

Of all the things it brings to mind—fish, water, or, for some people, an uncoiling snake—the one thing the BP Bridge does not bring to mind is an ordinary bridge. In the patently unlikely art of stretching weight-bearing structures across voids, strength combined with lightness has always been key to the architects' and engineers' solution. How to build a structure, unsupported for great lengths; how to make it strong, stable, and capable of carrying great loads? That has been the equation to crack over the centuries of bridge building. And the answer has always been to make that structure efficient, minimal, and as close to weightless as possible. The great bridge builders of the nineteenth and twentieth centuries—Robert Maillart, John Roebling, Alexandre-Gustave Eiffel, and Abraham Darby—achieved it with engineering methods that grew more and more sophisticated over time. Their famous bridges—the Salginatobel in rural Switzerland, the Brooklyn in New York, the Maria Pia in Porto, Portugal, and the Iron Bridge in Telford, Shropshire (England)—share an unadorned simplicity inspired by the need for lightness that led to an economy in materials. The disciplined exclusion of anything unnecessary gives each of these bridges the appearance of modernity.

The unique and formidable challenges of bridges, arguably greater than any skyscraper, continue to attract gifted architects and engineers. Santiago Calatrava and Lord Norman Foster are two contemporary architects who have reignited bridge design with deeply beautiful, imaginative work. A bridge commission is to an architect what an invitation to perform at Carnegie Hall is to a musician: an opportunity to measure one's work against the giants.

Challenge is surely part of what piqued Gehry's interest when Ed Uhlir showed him the master plan for Millennium Park in December 1998. "I've never done a bridge before," Gehry said. At the time, the commission for the bridge was not what Uhlir was in Gehry's Los Angeles office to discuss. He was there to ask Gehry to design the music pavilion. But Uhlir got the hint. Gehry would be more likely to take the music pavilion job if he got the bridge as well.

Redefining the bridge model

Typically, Gehry immediately redefined the challenge, turning the classic model of the bridge inside out and upside down. This bridge is anything but minimal. As is true of most of his work, this design is expressive. More promenade than straight march, this bridge carries viewers aloft and offers views from new and various vantage points. Blair Kamin, architecture critic for the *Chicago Tribune,* called it a "balcony to the bandshell." Kamin (whose early, mild published skepticism about the band-shell design made Gehry furious) continued his reverie on the completed bridge in a poetic vein, saying, "The curves in Frank's riverlike bridge form eddies where people stop to talk." Kamin recalled seeing "people hanging over the edge [of the bridge] and watching the orchestra play."

The social interaction and urban engagement the bridge inspires is, as Kamin suggests, partly a function of the bridge's excesses. Offering more than a mere means to cross the road, the BP Bridge offers us the city itself in a gorgeous panoramic view of Michigan Avenue, with Millennium Park in the foreground, as well as the perch from which to linger and enjoy it. Even Gehry is a little surprised by what he has done. "It's richer to see it with all the parts of the city. I didn't expect to have those views," he said.

For all its flourishes, the BP Bridge is also a functional structure, albeit surreptitiously so. This is not the functionalism signaled by taut cables, gleaming metal surfaces, and other high-tech elements in the architectural vocabulary. Rather, this is a functionalism as soft as this bridge's curves. In public spaces, accommodations for people with disabilities often appear as conspicuous add-ons: the ungainly cement ramp next to the graceful granite stairs.

That is partly because accessibility standards are relatively new to building codes, and adapting existing structures is difficult to do gracefully. But accessibility is integral to the BP Bridge design, and the effects are evident in the number of people in wheelchairs seen crossing the bridge along with everybody else. This is seamless design that leaves nobody outside the game. Early on, Gehry rejected a concept that would have made the bridge shorter but would have required elevators at each end to hoist people in wheelchairs up to and down from the crossing span. Instead, he chose to make the bridge long, folding it back and forth on itself, while gradually building up the slope (5 percent is the maximum slope for wheelchairs) to the height necessary to cross above Columbus Avenue. This solution also created the buffer to block traffic noise that would otherwise have interfered with performances at the Pritzker Pavilion. With his usual understatement, Gehry described the solution: "I strung out the ramp to use it as a sound barrier to the street. To give it scale and life, I wiggled it." All modesty aside, the achievement of consolidating good design with barrier-free design is enormous. This is true integration, not the afterthought that makes the wheelchair-bound feel like second-class citizens.

Bridge politics

Mayor Daley makes no secret of his opinions about architecture, and he did not like the design for the bridge. Gehry said, "I knew [the mayor] liked nineteenth-century architecture. . . . I knew he didn't want me to do the bridge, that was for sure." The mayor asked Gehry to meet with him in his office. Gehry went, and, as he talked, he picked up a pair of scissors from the mayor's table and used them to point to the bridge drawings. The mayor told Gehry he was afraid the strong bridge design would detract attention from the pavilion's stage.

They were looking at bird's-eye views of the bridge, and, from that angle, the bridge did look dominant. Gehry explained that, seen from the ground, the bridge would have a more subdued presence. Still, the mayor had reservations. Finally, after a dinner devoted to the topic of the BP Bridge with his wife, Maggie Daley, and John Bryan, the park's Art Committee chair and principal fund-raiser, Mayor Daley relented. Gehry, their taste differences notwithstanding, said that he likes and admires Mayor Daley, and he said he understands the mayor. "He's a control freak, like me," Gehry said.

Indeed, the sponsorship of the bridge by BP was the result of its own kind of politics. The gift for the bridge came when Lord John Browne was CEO of BP. Lord Browne had relationships in the United States and in Chicago going back many years, first as the head of the Standard Oil division after its acquisition by BP. Lord Browne served on the BP board when Amoco, then based in Chicago, was acquired by BP. Shortly thereafter Lord Browne became BP's CEO, his relationship to the States still in place.

Getting it done

As a pedestrian bridge of modest proportions, the BP Bridge is not breaking records on the terms for which bridges are usually celebrated—the length of its span or the novelty of its structural solution. Still, it presented considerable engineering and construction challenges. The trouble lay beneath the bridge. The west end of the bridge rests on the portion of Millennium Park's deck covering a parking garage; the east end rests on another covered garage—this one more than twenty-five years old; in between these points lies Columbus Drive. None of these structures had been built to support the weight of the proposed bridge. It was up to John Zils of SOM, the bridge's engineer, to find a way to get it done. Zils wanted to avoid the obvious and expensive solution of reinforcing the garages. In exchange for a five-foot layer of soil removed from the garage decks, Zils calculated that the east and west ends of the bridge could be borne as distributed weight on existing structures. Although it would have been more elegant, a clear, unsupported span over Columbus was out of the question. Without a compensating steadying support column, the curve in the bridge that is centered over the road is a torsion—or twisting force—that would topple the bridge. Further, to prevent vibrations from Columbus being transmitted through the center support column, it was threaded through existing substructures all the way down to the hardpan, a level of clay that lies on top of Chicago's bedrock.

To create the span, great box girders were pieced together, with the center section laid in last. The girders were cut and pieced together at the fabricator's Pittsburgh facility to ensure accuracy and fit before they were disassembled and shipped to Chicago. With the garage roofs fortified by additional, temporary supports, a 360-ton crane positioned on a closed Columbus Drive lifted the girders into place in an operation that lasted through the night.

The coiling ramps on the east and west ends of the bridge were fashioned with steel twenty-inch-diameter tubes. Once the structure was in place, the ninety-four hundred aluminum and stainless steel prefabricated shingles that form the cladding were placed one by one in their designated positions in a laborious, time-consuming process. "It was more like a house," said Zils. "[You] have a bridge with cladding like a building." With the ever-changing surface geometry of the bridge, the dimensions and curvature of each shingle had to be calculated using a sophisticated computer program called CATIA that Gehry's office has adapted from the aerospace industry to apply to architecture.

There are plenty of contradictions in Frank Gehry's work. This architect takes a tough industrial material like steel and treats it as though it were platinum, each piece of it individually formed and hand positioned. Steel—the stuff of industrial production lines—is the material Gehry chooses to return a measure of handicraft to the crude business of construction. Gehry also broods over multiple models of every project he undertakes, all in hopes of achieving the appearance of spontaneity. "I just . . . try to make it look casual, like, 'Look Ma, no hands,'" he said. He prefers buildings unfinished. "When they're under construction, they look great. Too bad they can't leave it like that," he said. That observation led him to ask himself, "How could a building be made to look like it's in process?" Then he is miffed when his laborious subterfuge succeeds. "People look at my work and think it's a soufflé and I just threw it together. I do a lot more careful work," he declares. The truth is that contradiction is the soul of Gehry's work. He turns shingles into scales. He makes crossing the street a journey. He makes architecture move.

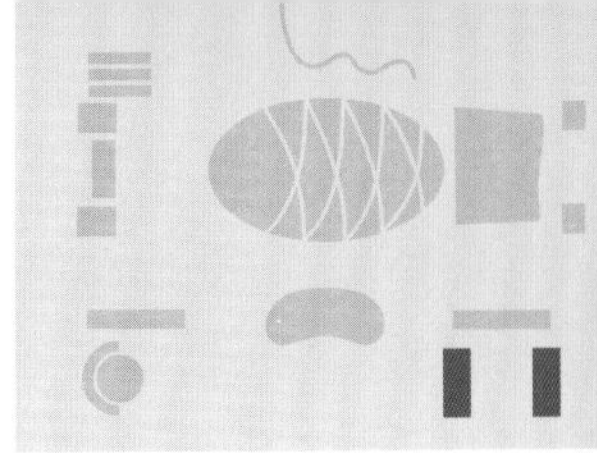

Crown Fountain

There is a huge emptiness in the piece that is inviting people to be there.

—JAUME PLENSA

Go to the Crown Fountain on a summer day and inevitably there are children, some who arrive in their bathing suits, acting out a drama they know by heart and seem never to tire of repeating. Two huge faces taking up the entire fifty-foot-tall facades of two glass towers appear to be looking at one another across a 230-foot-long plaza skimmed with a pool of water less than an inch deep. Kids play and chug around barefoot in the shallow water until suddenly they huddle together in two groups, one at either end of the pool, laughing and hugging themselves. At the same moment, the two projected faces on the glass towers change expression and from pursed lips emit spouts of water that fall exactly where the children have grouped. The kids laugh and scream. Soon, the projected water stops, the faces fade away, and the children hurry to stand against the base of the towers just as sheets of water spill down from the tower's top. This sequence is repeated over and over again, each time under the gaze of new faces looking out from the towers.

Even the artist who designed it, Jaume Plensa, was surprised by the reception his fountain received. "It will have to be unforgettable," Plensa said to himself when he was invited to compete for the Crown Fountain commission. He was up against two others, one of whom is the most prominent monument designer in the United States, and Plensa, although known in his native Spain and throughout Europe, was a relative newcomer. "I could never have imagined the way people adopted the piece."

The idea for the fountain

"He asked himself what a fountain could be," said Paul Gray of the Richard Gray Gallery, which represents Plensa in Chicago and New York. "He looked at the history of fountains, of meeting places, at why water is meaningful and its relationship to public spaces." As he considered his design, Plensa looked hard at one of the most famous and beautiful fountains in the world, Gian Lorenzo Bernini's 1651 Fountain of the Four Rivers in the Piazza Navona in Rome, with its enormous human figures representing the Ganges, the Nile, the Danube, and the Plate rivers. Plensa thought about the nature of water. "It is an elemental part of everything," he said. Equally important to him was creating a gathering place, a public square anchored by his fountain. "In Mediterranean cultures like mine, the square is very important. You could say, 'What is it? It is nothing. There is nothing there.' But the square is waiting for the people to come."

"My intention was to create something new and different," the artist said. "Finally, I decided on two houses with a black platform in between them, to create a space more than an object." And, unlike Bernini's heroic figures, Plensa said, "I wanted the real inhabitants of the city to be a part of it." The "gargoyles," as Plensa calls them, would be images of regular Chicagoans, and when those pictures appear to spout water from their mouths, the water represents an elemental gift. "Suddenly, they give you life," the artist said.

The patron and the architect

The scheme, together with Plensa's earnest charm, won over the Crown family and their arts advisers who selected him for the project. The Crowns would give the bulk of the $17 million it cost to build the fountain. But it was not initially clear how or whether the fountain could be built as it was designed by Plensa. The artist had worked with glass and created towerlike art pieces before, but he had done neither at the scale he proposed for this project.

The architectural firm Krueck & Sexton, which was known for its refined design and exacting execution of its buildings, was brought on the team. It would be up to the firm to figure out a way to build the fountain as Plensa had designed it. Plensa said, "Mark Sexton was the translator. He put my work into another language." It would be a more challenging charge than Sexton expected. "I think of this project as being like ballet because it looks effortless and it is really very difficult," he said.

Steven Crown understood that everything about the fountain was new and untried. He told Sexton, "You are going to fail, just don't fail on the final thing." In other words, the architect could experiment all he liked as long as he made the fountain work in the end. Every element of the fountain was tested to the point of failure. So, in September 2003 at the quarry in Italy where the granite for the plaza came from, a sample two-inch-thick stone tile was loaded with successively greater weight. It finally broke at ten thousand pounds—the weight of about three cars—over an area of three square inches. Both Crown and the architects were satisfied. So it was with every piece that went into the Crown Fountain.

The structure

When Plensa used glass blocks in other sculptures, he stacked them to create walls. With a tower equivalent in height to a five-story building, that method would not work. The tower could not be stable, and the glass at the base would shatter under the weight. Sexton devised an internal structure similar to one he would design for any building. It would distribute weight and take the force of the wind. The supporting structure is faintly visible through the glass. To Plensa, the structure was part of the fountain's "body"—it was appropriate that it be seen. Sexton agreed.

They felt otherwise about the gridded steel frame that holds each glass block in an individual compartment the way a carton from the grocery store cradles each egg. This frame was to be concealed from the observer by a special feature built into the glass. The frame is attached to the internal structure, and, aside from making it easy to replace broken blocks, it distributes the weight of the wall so it does not all fall to the bottom row of blocks. With a tolerance of just one sixteenth of an inch in alignment between the rows of glass blocks and the screens behind displaying the faces, the steel frame had to be—and was—fabricated with exactitude.

The glass

All 22,500 glass blocks used in the towers, plus a stockpile for replacing broken blocks, were hand cast at L. E. Smith, a small custom foundry near Pittsburgh. The best glass in the United States comes from around Pittsburgh as a lingering inheritance from the Czechs who immigrated to the United States and settled there. The ten-pound glass blocks were designed to have a small exterior lip to conceal the steel frame holding them in place. To the observer, the strength of the frame is concealed. The glass-block walls look like they are stacked one on top of another and grouted in place just like any ordinary load-bearing wall.

It took three craftspersons working together in a tightly choreographed minuet to make each glass block. The first would empty the ladle of five pounds of molten glass into a custom-made mold; the second would follow immediately behind with another ladle of equal weight. Evaluating the casting by eye alone, the third and most skilled craftsperson then snipped off the glass when he thought the block was at ten pounds. Working this way, the foundry could produce 350 blocks per day.

Through a series of prototypes, one important detail eluded the craftsmen and architects. That was finding the correct curve for the topmost tower blocks. Time and again they found that rather than sliding over, the water would shoot straight off the top. Far more than a nagging detail, getting this right meant the water would cascade, as intended, along the walls of the tower as it descended and as the artist planned. After six months' experimentation, they got it. Physics aided them. The natural attraction between surfaces works to keep the water adhering to or close to the tower walls: friction slows the water, reducing its force as it falls.

The spout

The team went to Toronto, Canada, in October 2003 for the first test of the fountain's spout. The water's force knocked down a two-hundred-pound man. There were aesthetic requirements: the water needed to look like a single, continuous stream, and it had to project a distance from the wall in a pleasing arc. In the end, Crystal Fountains devised something that met all the requirements and resembled a showerhead with small holes that stream the water together while reducing its force. It was made of transparent materials that render it nearly invisible.

The faces

If he could have chosen the fountain's neighbor, Plensa could not have picked a better one than the Art Institute of Chicago to ask for help. "The body was the physical part of the fountain and the soul was the face," Plensa said. "I asked, 'Who can do that soul?' The Art Institute is next door, and I thought maybe they could do it. It is like you need sugar and you go to your neighbor and ask, 'Can I have a cup of sugar?'" With an approach that was part science and part pure art, John Manning, an associate professor and video artist at the School of the Art Institute, took on the problem of realizing Plensa's vision precisely as the artist described it. "I wanted the fountain to represent the city, the largest mosaic of people, real people," Manning said.

Nothing like this had ever been done before on this scale using this technology. It would take two and a half years to create the catalog of faces and nature scenes, employing a camera previously used by George Lucas to shoot scenes for *Star Wars.* One thousand and fifty Chicagoans were videotaped, representing every religious group and ethnicity in the city; and every recording was digitized and manipulated by computer to achieve effects Plensa dictated.

Manning, who thought he would be an early adviser and nothing more, directed the project throughout with a staff that went from six to fifteen people depending on the stage of the project. Manning said, "I was one of the early video artists. . . . We had to build and repair our own equipment, so I understand the most arcane technical details." He was used to improvising and, as a fellow artist, was sympathetic to Plensa's intentions in a way that few others could be.

With the 2000 census data for Chicago, Manning's team, together with the assistance of the Department of Cultural Affairs, determined the groups that had to be represented to create what Manning calls "an archive of the people of Chicago." Next, Chicago community groups organized around race, age, and religious affiliations were searched out. There were nearly one thousand such groups. Letters went to all of them, asking for volunteers. Three hundred groups replied, and 150 of those were invited to select people to be videotaped. The selection was as random as the team could make it, the only criterion being inclusiveness.

"Video turns to mush," Manning said, when it is exploded to the dimensions of a fifty-foot-tall tower. So Manning used the best video camera available anywhere. Valued at $150,000, the camera records high-definition, panoramic images. To get the long, vertical images he needed, Manning simply turned the camera on its side and mounted it to a stable pedestal with an eight-inch-diameter suction cup of the type used in the film industry to attach cameras to cars for moving shots.

Originally, Manning wanted to tape each subject for thirteen minutes, but he quickly discovered that it was physically impossible for human beings to sit still for that long—an absolute requirement. To limit the subjects' natural inclination to fidget, Manning bought an old dentist's chair for $250. With its fixed headrest and adjustable height, all the subjects seated in it could be stabilized and positioned in the same posture and at the same height in relation to the immovable camera.

Each subject was taped for short periods two or three times. In one sequence, subjects were asked to simply hold still and look into the camera. For the second sequence, the subjects were to purse their lips as though they were blowing out a birthday candle. The latter images would be seamlessly appended to the first at the precise instant the jets of water are projected from the fountain. In the winter, when the water is not on, the second tape is omitted and the faces simply look out serenely at the world.

All the videotapes were digitized. From that moment forward, the work was done on computers. Each recording had to conform to certain requirements. "Everybody's eyes had to be in the same position, despite where Mother Nature put them," Manning said. The same was true of the mouths. A gridded template showing the boundaries for the features was laid over the images, and, using a computer animation program, the features were, as Manning said, "stretched like taffy until it all fit." Every five seconds, the image was checked to be certain each subject's features remained within the boundaries. If they shifted, the image was corrected. At the same time, the color of the images had to be adjusted in order for the faces to appear lifelike on the LED screens.

The team was close to having more data than it could handle. It built its own computer network, with fifteen large hard drives that could, together, contain the data for just 150 raw recordings at one time. Each face was moved off the network when modifying the features was completed.

Until the very end, there was no fifty-foot-tall LED screen to show the images, so the work remained fundamentally theoretical. An eight-by-ten-foot LED prototype was available to the team members a few times so they could test some images on a smaller scale. It was not until the towers were built just before the park's opening day that Plensa, Manning, and the entire team could be certain they had succeeded.

The screens

To decide who would make the LED screens displaying the faces on the towers, Sexton set up what he called a "shoot-out" between two candidates. Both made scaled mock-ups of the tower and constructed them in the alley behind the Krueck & Sexton offices. By this time, the team had taped some sample faces, and these were used for the test. Plensa, Crown, and Sexton were all there. LED screens are nothing more than superbright red, green, and blue lights, or pixels—many, many, many of them—turned on and off in rapid, sequenced combinations to create different colors and images. There is no lens and no projector used in this technology, a distinct virtue for the fountain. A Belgian company, Barco, was selected after the test.

The LED screens are assembled like tiles to create the large, single images at the fountain. There are 147 computers in each tower that feed the display data to screen modules measuring twenty-three by five inches. These modules are tied to large computer servers housed beneath the fountain orchestrating the randomized image selection, its display, and sequencing. The screens are placed close behind the glass wall and its frame. Because of the tight conditions, the LED screens had to be made accessible for maintenance and repairs from the back of the screen, inside the tower, rather than from the front, as is typical. The manufacturer struggled to resolve that problem for some time before finding a solution.

By the time the full-size display screens were completed, Plensa, Crown, Sexton, Manning, and others flew to Utah, where the manufacturer had a facility, so they could see the screens assembled and running. Barco had prevailed upon a neighboring amusement park, borrowing a roller coaster's structural system to temporarily support the enormous screen. There were tests to be done: the heat put out by the screens was measured, as was the light. They looked at the displayed images from seven hundred yards away and from up close. They spent the entire day there. Crown said, "We waited until dark before leaving for the airport. We could see it when we took off. There was the screen lighted up with a backdrop of mountains in a dark sky." It was going to work.

Construction schedule

With the design refined to the last detail and every element tested, the team was ready to start construction. The firm W. E. O'Neil would do the work. The long-lead items like the handmade glass, the custom LED screens, and the steel frame had been ordered and were ready to go. Then the team waited four months as lawyers worked out details and prepared to formally accept the Crown Fountain as a gift to the city of Chicago. The grand opening was to be July 23, 2004; the construction on the fountain was projected for completion in October 2004. It was conveyed to Crown that Mayor Daley "would really like the fountain to be ready for the opening, so we went into overdrive," Crown said. There was no time now to conceal construction behind tents or sheets of plastic so that the public would be surprised when the fountain was unveiled. Fortunately, the public was distracted by construction of Gehry's Pritzker Pavilion, so nobody paid much attention to the glass towers being erected at the southwest corner of the park. "We had to build, troubleshoot, and fix it at the same time," Crown said.

The team got it done just in time. The mayor was not able to push a button to turn the fountain on, as the team would have liked him to do on opening night. Once team members got the computers, the lighting, and the images up and running, they were afraid to turn them off in case they would not start up again on cue. Better safe than sorry, they thought, and kept the fountain going once it was up. Although the plan was to turn off the fountain sometimes, everyone in the city became accustomed to having it going 24/7, and that is how it has been ever since.

All the planning

A least one of the Crown Fountain's features was serendipitous. As the artist originally planned it, the water plaza between the two glass towers was to have been just one-eighth of an inch deep, the thinnest skim/skin of water that would have produced a reflective black granite surface contrasting with the dry, matte-black granite on the rest of the plaza, while still creating the humid, cooling conditions Plensa wanted. In any case, the artist imagined people "walking on water" so shallow they could have kept their shoes on. Because it was not technically possible to ensure that such a thin coating of water would cover the space between the towers and cover it evenly, the depth was increased. With that change, the only way to walk on this water is to take off your shoes or reconcile yourself to ruining them. That's when the kids took over Crown Fountain.

EXELON PAVILION

Exelon Pavilions

The success of Millennium Park had a deep and sincere effect on the [Art Institute's] trustees.

—JAMES CUNO

Italian architect Renzo Piano made his first leap across Monroe Street to Millennium Park when he designed the two Exelon Pavilions using the same strategy and materials he had used in the new Modern Wing of the Art Institute of Chicago.

The north and south walls of the pavilions are opaque, made of textured Indiana limestone—stone from the same quarry as that which clads the museum addition—while the east and west walls are glass. (Exceptionally transparent, the glass is made with very little iron.) At the museum, where art needs to be shielded from direct light, the design promises to provide the necessary protection while permitting natural light to illuminate the work. The pavilions—one at the southeast corner of the park and the second directly opposite the museum addition—offer access to the parking garages below.

Piano made a second, much longer jump to the park when his design for the 625-foot Nichols Bridgeway connected the museum addition directly to the park. The pedestrian bridge begins near the center of the park and climbs 60 feet to the third story of the Modern Wing. Along the way it offers views to Lake Michigan to the east and the Loop to the west from a wholly new vantage point. Before the bridge was named for its benefactors, Piano called it "The Blade," a term that captures the bridge's extremely thin, elegant form.

On Randolph Street along the park's northern edge are two more pavilions, also named for and funded by Exelon, the corporate parent to Commonwealth Edison. These make the relationship between structure and benefactor explicit. Both are arresting, completely black reflective buildings that, on closer examination, reveal themselves to be covered entirely in photovoltaic cells that capture energy from the sun and funnel it into the city's power grid. The Welcoming Center is housed in the pavilion just west of the Harris Theater. The second pavilion on Randolph is east of the Harris and provides access to the parking garage below. Intended as a demonstration project by Exelon, the solar towers were executed by Hammond Beeby Rupert Ainge.

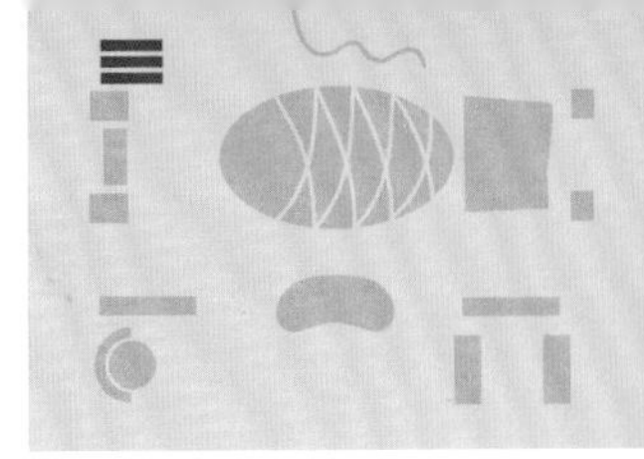

McDonald's Cycle Center

This was not your everyday project.

—CYNTHIA MULLER

For a tiny building, the bike station at Millennium Park harbors large ambitions. As an example of environmentally conscious, "green" architecture and a facility for car-shunning commuter bicyclists, the station is environmentally conscientious through and through.

The station was a latecomer to the park, as was its sponsor, McDonald's, a local company with an interest in associating itself with healthy activities. With a City of Chicago program promoting bicycling, the decision to keep Millennium Park purely pedestrian, although appropriate to the park's atmosphere, begged accommodation. The first thought was to dedicate a plaza in the park to bike racks. That proposal was nixed as too messy. So, like most things in Millennium Park, the station evolved, becoming ever more ambitious and, finally, precedent setting.

By the time planners were through, the station had become the first in the country to offer the range of amenities it does, including showers and locker rooms, in an architecturally and environmentally ambitious building. The station provides subscribing cyclists with a secure, protected place to park during their visit to Millennium Park. Supporting a dedicated group of cyclists who bike to work, it is a demonstration project showing how one urban alternative to commuting by car could work.

There is room to store three hundred bicycles in a supervised space at the station.

Members pay a fee for access to the showers and locker rooms and, using a pass card, can come and go as they like before, after, and during normal operating hours. Original estimates projected that just forty people would sign up for membership in the first year. Instead, memberships sold out. The Chicago Police Department's Bicycle Patrol Unit is based at the station.

The bulk of the station is housed below the plaza at Randolph Street and Columbus Drive, nested in the parking garage structure that underlies Millennium Park. It is visible from the street only as a small, two-story glass and steel atrium with an angled roof and bright awnings.

Janet Attarian, an architect with the Chicago Department of Transportation, managed the project. She chose Chicago architects Muller+Muller to design the station because, having done several infrastructure projects, they were accustomed to working with the city, and Attarian knew they could design well in the modern idiom she felt was most appropriate to the job.

Attarian worked with design architect David Steele to develop the plan. The space allocated to the station descends three and a half stories. Laying it out took cunning. Ramps are the best means to meet accessibility standards and to negotiate bikes through level changes, but they eat up space. Attarian co-opted the public, surface plaza behind the building site as her ramped entryway, thus saving some interior space. A path looping behind the building and down one story leads to the entry for bike parking. A second entry to the building is provided by stairs from the plaza, with a trough running parallel to it for wheeling down bicycles.

Impressed by a green European building where

solar cells had been left exposed to create a visible pattern, Attarian decided to try a similar concept at the bike station. The glass roof is angled to the south to efficiently capture the maximum sunlight throughout the year. The photovoltaic cells are applied in a pattern that can be read inside the building. They cast a handsome dappling shadow inside.

Steele came up with another device. Cables strung a distance from the exterior walls between the ground and the roof support plants that grow through the spring and summer. In the warm months, the plants block direct sunlight from penetrating the south and east faces of the building. In the winter, when the plants are dormant, the sun gets through and helps keep the building warm. The energy generated by the building is fed into the city's power grid, and the station is credited its value.

Working on a hurry-up, three-month schedule just before the park opened, Attarian recalls counting eighty-eight workers employed on the site at one point. The building cost $2.9 million, $1 million of which came from a federal grant program dedicated to pollution-reducing projects and the balance from the State of Illinois. Being shoehorned into the existing garage structure meant the bike station had to accommodate its surroundings. Everything in the building had to be custom-made for its purpose. There were also engineering issues. A consultant was hired to safely accommodate an existing twenty-foot-thick support beam in the garage with the new construction. Attarian and Steele selected materials and finishes for the interiors that they knew were available and could be delivered quickly. Glass tiles from Italy were last to arrive, causing some last-minute anxiety. The bike station opened on schedule with the rest of Millennium Park. Between 8:00 and 9:00 A.M. on a spring morning, purposeful commuting bikers are busily coming and going, and tourists are trying out the rentals.

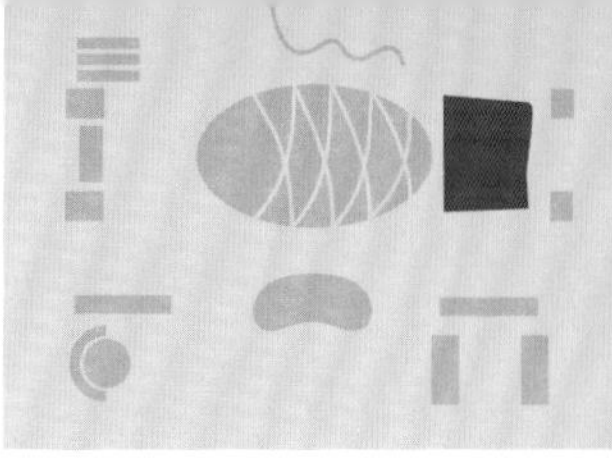

Lurie Garden

Some people have never seen a bee on a bloom before.

—COLLEEN SCHUETZ

Vigilant and oblivious: these are the contrary twin states of mind every big-city dweller cultivates. Ignore the taxicab's honking, unless it's about to hit you. Focus on your book, but do not miss your train stop. So it may take a moment or two in the Lurie Garden to suspend the automatic urban defense system. This garden means to engage and please all the senses. There is the faint sound of water lapping, unseen, beneath the boardwalk that bisects the garden and the water's cooling breath on feet and legs as it rises through the boards. There is the barely detectable scent of limestone moistened by water. In the spring and summer, there are bees and butterflies to see. From the hedge where they have secreted themselves come the sounds of insects. And, of course, there are the plants, flowering and nonflowering, to see and smell, to hear rustling in the breeze. You are in a meadow at the corner of Monroe Street and Columbus Drive, in the heart of downtown Chicago.

Roy Diblik still can't believe it. "To find those plants on Michigan Avenue . . . ten years ago they would have been out there with weed whips," he said. Diblik has been passionate for years about the native midwestern perennials that account for many of the plantings in the Lurie Garden. Working with the project's master plantsman in the Netherlands, Piet Oudolf, Diblik raised many of the plants in the garden on his farm in Wisconsin. Diblik was one member of a team assembled from around the globe to make a garden that is at once radically new and utterly emblematic of Chicago and its past.

The competition

Many contemporary landscape designers think of their work the way artists think of sculpture or painting—media that can be shaped to express fundamental, often abstract messages. Unlike nineteenth-century picturesque parks and gardens that re-created idealized versions of nature, radical new landscapes insist on announcing their artificiality with anything from synthetic surfaces, such as rubber, to constructed landforms, such as geometrically uniform rolling earth waves covered in grass. Or, as in the Lurie Garden, a new landscape can do both of these things: it can convincingly evoke a country meadow with blowing grasses and wildflowers from its perch atop a concrete parking garage.

The elevated ambitions that were reshaping parts of Millennium Park were contagious. Expectations for the garden rose too. The original Beaux Arts master plan had become a backdrop for radical new work, and an early classical design for the garden had been discarded. Instead, a competition for the garden inviting the world's best contemporary landscape designers to participate was organized by Ed Uhlir. He asked for a new design appropriate for a park celebrating the arrival of the twenty-first century. A $200,000 grant from the Richard H. Driehaus Foundation would pay for the competition, including $10,000 stipends for each design firm.

Among the competitors were Dan Kiley and Laurie Olin, each of whom had designed one of the gardens on Michigan Avenue flanking the Art Institute of Chicago. Some argued that Kiley or Olin would create a strong design link between a new garden and the neighboring museum. "We already have a Kiley and an Olin," Uhlir argued. He wanted someone new.

The competition required more work than the $10,000 stipend would cover. Kathryn Gustafson and her Seattle partners, Jennifer Guthrie and Shannon Nichol—their firm is Gustafson Guthrie Nichol Ltd., or GGN—debated whether they should enter. "We try to look at the client," Gustafson said. "Are they serious? Can they afford it? What is the local political situation? Can the mayor get things done?" The answers were all favorable. What proved most persuasive, however, Gustafson said, was that the City of Chicago "really wanted to do something original." The partners decided to enter.

Gustafson was sitting at her kitchen table at her home outside Seattle; she had just received the short list for the Lurie Garden competition. Her office was one of three finalists. However, a name she expected to see was not there. That was Piet Oudolf, the Dutch designer internationally famous for composing four-season gardens inspired by the thought that perennials are as beautiful in decline as they are in bloom. Indeed, Oudolf is a leader in introducing this philosophy to the world of landscape design and horticulture. His work composing plantings is expressed in a delicate, painterly, infinitely subtle manner. Although he had been invited to compete, Oudolf thought the project too large for his office and had not participated. As Gustafson reached for the telephone, it started ringing. Oudolf, whom she had intended to call, was on the line. Uhlir had suggested Oudolf contact her.

Gustafson and Oudolf already knew one another through lectures both had given in London. Over the telephone, they agreed to collaborate on the Lurie Garden. With Oudolf on the team, GGN sought a Chicago partner to help oversee the garden's execution. Terry Guen Design Associates was selected. Guen's firm would also design the plantings for the interstitial spaces connecting the major features to one another throughout Millennium Park.

Gustafson has an unusual background. She is American, a former fashion designer who worked in New York and Paris and became a landscape architect after training at the École Nationale Supérieure du Paysage at Versailles in France. She has practices in Seattle and London and extensive experience in Europe, where experimental landscape design has been welcomed for decades. She is known for sculptural landscapes that express qualities unique to each site she designs. One of her best-known works is the Diana, Princess of Wales Memorial Fountain in London. It is an irregular circular channel with water flowing through at changing densities and speeds as it descends. Likened to a necklace tossed on the ground, it has been interpreted as an expression of the princess's tempestuous spirit, as symbolic of the English landscape through which water runs to the Thames River, and as a pure abstract exploitation of water's sensual qualities.

Smart, down-to-earth, and generous, Gustafson is quick to credit her partners and her team. "When everyone collaborates, everyone needs a piece they can call their own," she said. She is also protective. When Piet Oudolf, a soft-spoken man who seems not to relish life's complications, could not manage the remote for the slide projector at a public presentation of the Lurie Garden, it was Gustafson who rushed from her chair onstage to his side to help him.

The design

"This paper has traveled quite a bit," Gustafson said, referring to the garden design drawings. When Gustafson had to be in London, Guthrie traveled there from Seattle so the two could work together on the design. Later there were meetings as well with Oudolf in Chicago and in Seattle, where the designers brought their work to the table. "The basic concept was that each of us would go off and practice our expertise. We were all coming from different cities and continents. You need these meetings to be physically together," Gustafson said, "so you can see the other person and see what is important to them. You integrate those things that are important to each person."

Gustafson considered what surrounded the site and how the new garden would be used. The overall design, for which GGN was responsible, would have to respond to these conditions. Even though it is in the very heart of the city, there is openness around the garden. There was Grant Park on one side and the Pritzker Pavilion's Great Lawn on another side. The Art Institute of Chicago, its coming addition, and the wall of buildings on Michigan Avenue were the large masses. Gustafson concluded that the garden, like its surroundings, needed to be "open and it needed to be dense and full."

Gustafson starts designing by making lists of significant words and phrases. Two on the list stayed with her. One was the "City of Big Shoulders," from Carl Sandburg's famous 1914 poem "Chicago," and the second was the expression "I will." Through an understanding of

Chicago's history, Gustafson was forming an image of the city she would express in her design. She saw Chicago as it was at first, a marsh, and then as a determined, hardworking city that could raise itself after the catastrophic Great Chicago Fire of 1871 and reinvent itself by claiming land from Lake Michigan.

She sculpted a model in clay of the 2.5-acre site that evoked this character and narrative. Surprisingly, 50 percent of GGN's work is built on concrete, just as the Lurie Garden is, which presents technical problems but is also paradoxically liberating. The designer is inventing a landscape, and any sculptural form is valid as long as it works. "With constructed land you try not to pretend it is anything other than what it is. There is no pretext of naturalness," Gustafson said. She decided the garden would be divided into four major zones: the Shoulder Hedge, the Light Plate, the Dark Plate, and the Seam. Each zone is characterized by its own topography, plantings, and exposure to natural light, and each evokes a Chicago story. Gustafson said it wouldn't matter if no one ever understood the allusions underlying the Lurie Garden design. That it works as a garden is the important thing. The history she used to find her way to the design is the stuff of inspiration, the theme she used to give shape and coherence to the garden.

Because she was thinking about the new Art Institute galleries overlooking the Lurie Garden, Gustafson said, "I tilted the garden plane toward the Art Institute—it's like raking the seats in a theater so you can see the dancers' feet—the garden will be like a living painting changing through the seasons."

The Shoulder Hedge

The Pritzker Pavilion and its curling, silver, steel tresses appear balanced like a head on the massive Shoulder Hedge, as Gustafson named this feature at the north end of the Lurie Garden, in reference to Sandburg's famous phrase, "City of the Big Shoulders." When the hedge grows in completely, it will form a geometric wall of changing colors—there are both evergreens and deciduous plantings—wrapping the end of the Great Lawn. This wall is broken only by entry to the three principal pathways through the garden. Although the garden is generally the most peaceful area in Millennium Park, when concerts are ending at the pavilion, as many as eleven thousand people track quickly through it on their way to park exits. On these occasions, the hedge acts as a sentinel wall shielding the delicate planted beds of perennials that stand between it and the exits. Large crowds are effectively deflected by the hedge along the major paths to the exits without disturbing the garden. In time, the metal armature that resembles a great cage will disappear into the greenery as the hedge fills out. Then it will begin serving its real function as a cutting guide for the garden caretakers. Devices such as this have been used to shape topiary since the French king Louis XIV's garden at Versailles was designed in the seventeenth century by André Le Nôtre. Until the Shoulder Hedge finishes growing in, about 2015, the outline it will ultimately assume is precisely defined in bronze-colored steel. "Louis XIV had to wait for his garden too," Gustafson said.

The Light Plate

There are no sheltering trees here, and the sunlight comes down bright and unobstructed on the irregularly shaped perennial beds in the Light Plate. This zone has multiple meanings for Gustafson. She sees it as representing the bright and flourishing future of Chicago. But she also means to bring history to mind, recalling the midwestern prairie and "the light on the top of the world, as it was on the Great Plains." Ninety percent of the plants are native in this area of the garden. "That is how close I could come to nature in the city," said Oudolf. He also said it is the most complex part of the garden. Changes in height among the beds have been dramatized using plantings. A small rise appears lofty when topped, for example, by tall grasses, and plants at path edges that are small and finely detailed can seem magnified. This zone is likely to be most inviting in autumn and spring when the direct light from the south will be warming. In summer, it is hot, in winter, cold. The planting beds are angled upward slightly as though rising out of eagerness for the direct southern sunlight. Narrow paths with fine gravel permit visitors to get close-up views of the plantings. Benches are nestled into slots cut into the edge of the Shoulder Hedge that forms the south boundary of the Light Plate.

The Dark Plate

Light on the Dark Plate will become dappled as the trees grow in. Gustafson imagines this area recalling Chicago before the fire. "This is more about texture and that abundance of vegetation," she said. Here the paths are cut below the plane of the beds so the visitor's eye is closer to the plants; there is a feeling of being enveloped by the landscape. The trees were selected for their leaf patterns and because they branch horizontally, so they will create a canopy over time. There are redbuds, two types of cherry trees, and the hardy, native black

locust, with its faint vanilla fragrance. The wooden benches are like tables, low and wide so as not to interfere with views of the plantings. The light fixtures were custom-made. This zone is likely to attract visitors in summer when it is hot and in winter when a sheltering windbreak will be welcomed.

The Seam

The Seam, with its long boardwalk balanced over a pool of water, divides the Dark and Light Plates from one another and forms a major path through the garden. To Gustafson, the Seam is symbolically rich, representing the moving shore of Lake Michigan as it was filled to create parkland in the early part of the twentieth century. The designer dropped a platform to one side of the boardwalk and just below so people can sit and put their feet in the water if they like. They do. Narrow bridges cross the channel to other parts of the garden.

The winner and runners-up

Sunny Fischer, executive director at the Driehaus Foundation, recalls the public reaction to the designs when they were exhibited at the Chicago Cultural Center across the street from the Millennium Park site. "You could see people gathering around the Kathryn Gustafson scheme, it was just so interesting," Fischer said. Ed Uhlir would have been happy to stop right there. After he saw the GGN submission, he said, "I didn't think we needed a second competition stage. But I was only a consultant to the jury." He was sold.

There were two other finalists: Dan Kiley and Jeff Mendoza. Kiley's was a crisp, modernist scheme of a piece with other work in his much-admired portfolio and lengthy career. Kiley, who died in 2004 at age ninety-one, had ordered his plan with a grid and an on-center processional walkway and an allée of trees. Mendoza's was titled "Urban Riff" and was also organized by a grid as an ironic nod (unlike Kiley's, which was not ironic in any sense) from the designer to the organizing principle of most American cities. Mendoza disrupted his grid with an irrational overlay of curves and subdivided plots alluding to this country's dynamism and resistance to homogeneity.

Interesting as they were, the two runners-up had neither the topographic texture nor the complexity of experience the GGN scheme contained. The winning design promised that visitors would walk through a continuously changing landscape where varying perspectives offered new views. The runners-up were single ideas expressed well; the winner was a contained universe.

Ann Lurie, for whose family the garden is named, donated $10 million to the garden and an endowment for its upkeep. Lurie is a philanthropist with broad interests in the arts, health care, and social causes. "She's the real angel," Diblik said.

The plantings

Piet Oudolf visited Roy Diblik's perennials farm in 2001 and knew he had found the right place. Oudolf wanted unusual plants for the Lurie Garden, and to get them, he needed to find someone near Chicago to grow them. The men began a two-and-a-half-year collaboration. Diblik grew the most unusual plants for the garden himself and supervised other planters supplying more conventional ones. There are 140 varieties and a total of thirty thousand perennial plants in the Lurie Garden.

Often, landscape designers send plant lists out for bid to wholesale nurseries, and the winner, when it comes time to actually do the planting, substitutes plants it has in stock for those actually requested. "They promise, and then they substitute," Diblik said. "If this had gone out for bid, Piet would never have gotten what he wanted." It is rare to grow specific plants from seed and to have time to develop the palette as fully as Oudolf did. Oudolf sent seeds from the Netherlands to Diblik in Wisconsin to plant and to see if they would flourish in the midwestern climate. And Oudolf's refinements were extremely delicate. Because he wanted tonal color differences among the stems of the echinacea, for example, Oudolf sent seeds for two nonstandard varieties, which Diblik grew for him. These two are in the garden, along with the standard echinacea. For his part, Diblik introduced Oudolf to native plants, some of which—including a wild petunia that blooms in late July—were incorporated into the garden.

With all his cultivation, planning, and analysis, what Oudolf is trying to achieve is a facsimile of the natural world. "What is important in my work is bringing back that feeling of the wild," he said. To do it, "you have to understand what the plants will do. You have to understand the climate." He is like a conductor: "Every season should have its leading plants." In May, June, and July, the Lurie has a "blue river" running through it. This is, he said, "the first highlight of the season." In August, the orchestration calls for pink and purple to come to the fore.

Oudolf is passionate about appreciating the full span of a plant's life. He said, "I think the beauty of a plant is not over when it declines. It's bringing back the dynamics of the seasons. . . . Perennials, they have all these performances through the seasons. They come out, they live, they flower, they die beautifully, and they come back beautifully. It's a dynamic process, and you have all these things to experience in one season." At times, Oudolf seems nearly overwhelmed by the beauty and complexity of what he does. "It is very hard," he says gravely and often when he describes his work.

Creating a garden is setting a process in motion, and the best designer looks far into the future. The plants need to be considered together as neighbors and families. "Compatible means not competing with other plants, not driving them out. Plants need to be competitive only in that they are all equally strong," Oudolf explained. Nor do you want seeding plants that will pop up all around. "Nonaggressive and nonseeding is what you want. These qualities are essential to keep a garden as it is," Oudolf said.

Construction and planting

For all the time the team had to develop its scheme and grow the plants, the construction schedule was tight and the site unaccommodating. The Lurie Garden site was being used to store materials for the Pritzker Pavilion during its construction. With just a little more than a year before Millennium Park's opening day, the contractors who would build the garden gained access to the site in August 2003. Even then, Jennifer Guthrie, the GGN partner who was project manager for the garden, did not have critical "as-built" drawings showing the exact conditions on her site. A survey was done. Guthrie also relied on Uhlir.

He knew more details than anyone about the deck she would be building on and the garage beneath it.

For a time, the team had two gates through which to bring in supplies. But as soon as the pavilion and the BP Bridge were completed, the Columbus Drive gate was closed, leaving just one at Monroe Street with tightly restricted hours. With almost no room on the site to keep materials, access was critical. Twice, Ozgur Gocmen, assistant project manager for Walsh Construction, found himself in the backseat of a police squad car for unloading materials outside the prescribed hours. "We paid some fines," he said.

In anticipation of a garden on the southwest corner, Millennium Park planners and engineers had specified construction of a deck that would withstand the heavy weight of soil, trees, and other materials. They had allowed for the weight of four feet of soil spread over the surface, a sufficient depth to grow trees. The soil depths vary over the garden as circumstances require. Where there are trees, the soil is four feet deep. Shrubs need thirty inches; the perennials require eighteen to twenty-four inches. For each plant type, the amount of soil it needed to flourish—and no more—was provided. A superlight, strong material resembling Styrofoam was used beneath the soil to achieve height without adding weight. This material, called geofoam, comes in blocks of eight by four feet and was pieced together over the garden like a three-dimensional puzzle to make the level changes Gustafson planned. Geofoam covers 85 percent of the garden and at its highest point is forty inches thick.

To understand the complexity of the task of distributing weight in the garden, consider this. For a single, small tree, the engineers needed to know the weight of such a tree at maturity, perhaps twenty years out, as well as the weight of the materials required to support it—the soil and the water that would nourish it. Knowing all this, the engineers would have to verify that the tree was placed where it would be supported, along with its human visitors—perhaps one, perhaps hundreds. Throughout construction and planting, Guthrie said, her project engineers were checking and calculating to be certain the weight on the deck was within tolerances.

The contractors divided the site into quadrants, beginning at the northeast corner and moving counterclockwise. Workers began by applying a hot rubberized material to the surface to make it waterproof. Cold weather caused the first delays when ice made it impossible to seal parts of the surface. The narrow, open seams, called expansion joints, built into the deck to accommodate natural contraction and swelling in the concrete through the extremes of winter and summer cycles had to be redesigned so they would also be waterproof. Over the waterproofing, workers spread a four-inch-thick layer of gravel, called structural soil, for drainage. Then came the foam layer and, on top of that, the soil.

The Seam, with its three-hundred-foot-long pool—perhaps the most beloved element in the Lurie Garden—was the most complicated and costly part of the construction. "Most people would not have done that," Gustafson said. "There is no visual premium." With its boardwalk suspended over a gently circulated pool of water, more sensory dimensions enter the garden. "We worked that detail really hard," Gustafson said. The effect is delicate, but the means of achieving it are brutal and real-world. Electrical pumps in the parking garage push the water up three stories to the pool, where it is circulated through seventy jets embedded in the east wall of the pool.

At the beginning of June 2004, with Millennium Park's opening just six weeks away, Piet Oudolf arrived to plant the perennials with Diblik. Oudolf did the most complicated garden first, the Light Plate on the west side of the Lurie, making minor modifications as he went. Next, he planted the Dark Plate on the east side of the Seam. It took just one week. With no time for the plants to fill out, the plantings looked thin that first summer. "After

BorgWarner
Santa Fe

two years, most gardens are good," Oudolf said. The second summer, the garden was transformed; it looked promising; the third year, it was fully beautiful and robust.

The last tradespeople on the site were the ironworkers who built the cagelike cutting guide for the Shoulder Hedge. Near the end of the project, Gocmen said, there was no place at all to store either building or plant materials. Big trucks carrying the limestone used to edge the planting beds and face the walls of the pool were arriving nearly every day. At the same time, delicate plants were arriving to be carried into the garden by hand and by wheelbarrow.

Caring for the Lurie Garden

It is rare for a public garden to have its own steward. But with the $10 million gift from the Ann and Robert H. Lurie Family Foundation, an endowment was created that supports the garden's upkeep. Horticulturist Colleen Schuetz oversees the garden, and she has the freedom to quickly replace plants that have not thrived or to make other adjustments. She consults with Piet Oudolf. "I designed it, but you care for it," Oudolf said to Schuetz when they met at the opening celebrations. Oudolf returns annually. "It's like someone updating an artwork," said Diblik.

Schuetz is a rare creature, an extroverted horticulturist who likes people as much as plants. She has devised tours and other programs for the public that explain why the Lurie Garden is special. From the many people who have volunteered to work in the garden, she has chosen a core group of Master Gardeners—a title awarded to people who complete a difficult, prescribed gardening course—to help her maintain it.

A meadow in the middle of a busy city seems, on the face of it, odd. But Schuetz sees a natural aesthetic relationship. "The buildings and the plants are both tall, and narrow and upright. The buildings make the garden look better, and the garden makes the buildings look better." Beyond the science of horticulture, Schuetz gets the essence of this place and its value to Chicago's residents. "I believe in it. Some people have never seen a bee on a bloom before," she said. That may be the most important legacy she looks after: the spirit and value of this unlikely place.

WITH ENDURING GRATITUDE TO LEADING INDIVIDUALS, CORPORATIONS AND FOUNDATIONS FOR THEIR GENEROUS GIFTS

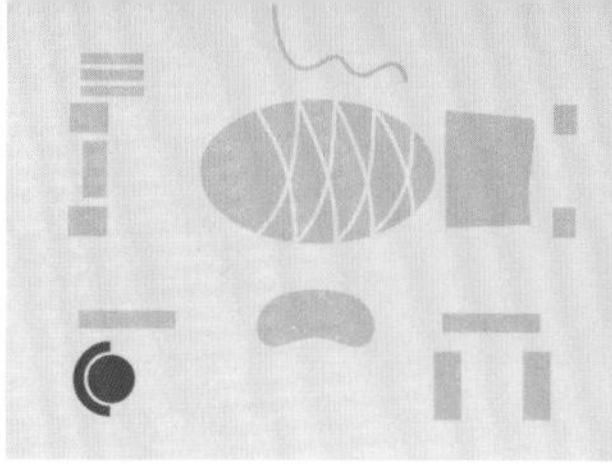

Millennium Monument at Wrigley Square

Slowly it all changed.

—THOMAS BEEBY

In a park dedicated to the future, one corner tidily connects two distant points on Chicago's time line. The Millennium Monument at Wrigley Square is a near re-creation of the structure that stood on the same spot between 1917 and 1953. The original's classical styling alluded to the great European parks that were models for Grant Park. The rebuilt reincarnation restores that reference and adds a contemporary notation. Inscribed in the base are the names of the people and organizations who together contributed more than $220 million to Millennium Park's construction.

The monument stands where one of Chicago's oldest parks once was. Before a series of landfill operations, when Michigan Avenue still marked the shoreline, the southeast corner of Randolph Street and Michigan Avenue was a part of Lakefront Park, a thin ribbon of property declared public land as early as 1835. The park was enlarged eastward with landfill over the years to create Grant Park.

Architect and planner Edward H. Bennett designed the original peristyle, upon which the current monument is modeled, in the style advanced in the 1909 Plan of Chicago, which he had worked on with Daniel Burnham. In 1953, the peristyle was knocked down so work could begin on the parking garage below Michigan Avenue. A newspaper account of the

demolition quoted the Chicago Park District's general superintendent, George Donoghue, as saying, "It's going to be modernistic along Michigan. Those Greek columns just wouldn't fit in. They are just too old-fashioned for the Chicago of tomorrow."

The "Chicago of tomorrow," as it turned out, regretted the loss and rebuilt the classically inspired peristyle curves around a fountain and pool in an environment where it coexists with the landmark architectural district across the street, the adjacent radical architecture of Frank Gehry, and the avant-garde sculpture of Anish Kapoor.

With only photographs, partial original plans, and drawings from archives available to him, the architect Michael Sullivan of O'Donnell Wicklund Pigozzi & Peterson could not replicate the design. His version, which has a smaller site, is about 80 percent of the scale of the original. The columns on the original were forty feet high, as compared to the thirty-six-foot-tall columns of the new monument. The base on the present version is also higher to accommodate the donors' engraved names. A ramp for handicap access, not a part of the original design, wraps around the back of the monument and leads to an elevated terrace.

In an upgrade, the new peristyle is made of French and Indiana limestone, rather than the formed concrete of the original. The detailed relief carving on the upper part of the monument was done by hand by the Bybee Stone Company in Bloomington, Indiana. That company, which is renowned for its artisans, uses traditional techniques. When the architects sent detailed drawings of the monument to the company as three-dimensional computerized drawings, the artisans converted the drawings to two dimensions, a format that contains less information but is the one in which they were accustomed to working. Some of the carved patterns on the cornice are antique. The "egg-and-dart" sequence of ovals and arrowhead shapes, for example, is found here and ornamenting the Pantheon in Rome, built between 118 and 128 A.D. Other patterns Sullivan incorporated, such as the Y that represents the Chicago River, are specific to this design and location.

The nozzle in the fountain is a subtle acknowledgment of the William Wrigley Jr. Foundation, the donor organization that made the monument and Wrigley Square possible. It is a cast-bronze duplicate of the finials on the ebullient white corporate headquarters only a few blocks north on Michigan Avenue, on the north side of the Chicago River.

The monument at Wrigley Square was one of the earliest elements in Millennium Park to be completed, and its traditional styling reflects that. More than anything in the park, this installation reflects the original Beaux Arts plan SOM originally designed. While elements of that plan remain in the interstitial areas and at Wrigley Square, the radical revisions and the sponsors' changed ambitions are reflected in the Pritzker Pavilion, Crown Fountain, *Cloud Gate,* and the Lurie Garden.

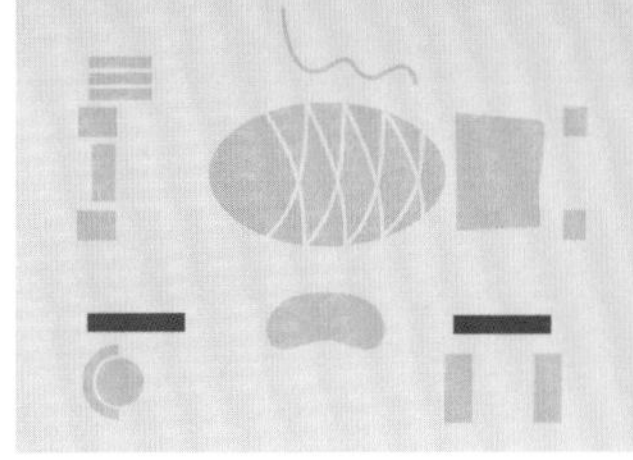

Boeing Galleries

Millennium Park turns Grant Park into a Beaux Arts park with a lot less starch in its collar.

—BLAIR KAMIN

Located on midlevel terraces on the north and south sides of Millennium Park, the Boeing Galleries are like outdoor rooms where rows of fragrant sycamore trees act as the walls. Like most conventional museum galleries, these are designed as noncompeting backdrops for the changing contemporary art exhibits on display from year to year in the park and the major park features linked through the galleries.

The galleries are formal, with straight lines, symmetrical plantings, and open, central paved aisles for displaying art. The galleries are intended as quiet foils to the park's assertive features, such as the Pritzker Pavilion. Destination places when art is on exhibit, the galleries assume a different role when art is not being shown, when they function purely as passages through the park. In that capacity, these are the restful, shaded places to stroll after taking in *Cloud Gate,* the Lurie Garden, or the Crown Fountain. They are like mints after a big dinner.

The south gallery establishes a connection with the Crown Fountain, which it overlooks, by using the same dark granite for its paving as the fountain's plaza. But the connection is understated, a device to create harmony between the two zones. (The two are connected literally by a concrete staircase in the style used throughout the park.) The north gallery works in a similar way, with its classicism complementing Wrigley Square's historical character.

Bloodgood sycamore—also known as the London plane tree—was chosen for the Boeing Galleries because of its full, round canopy; its picturesque, peeling bark; and its scent. The Bloodgood adapts well to urban environments and is known to be resistant to diseases that plague other varieties of sycamore trees. Although these trees stand in some of the great European parks, and one is said to be the oldest living tree in New York's Central Park, they have been rare in Chicago until now.

The galleries were funded by a $5 million gift from the Boeing Corporation.

EXIT
2
4 UPPER LOBBY
3 UPPER BALCONY
2 LOWER BALCONY
1 ORCHESTRA
2
4 UPPER LOBBY
3 UPPER BALCONY
2 LOWER BALCONY
1 ORCHESTRA

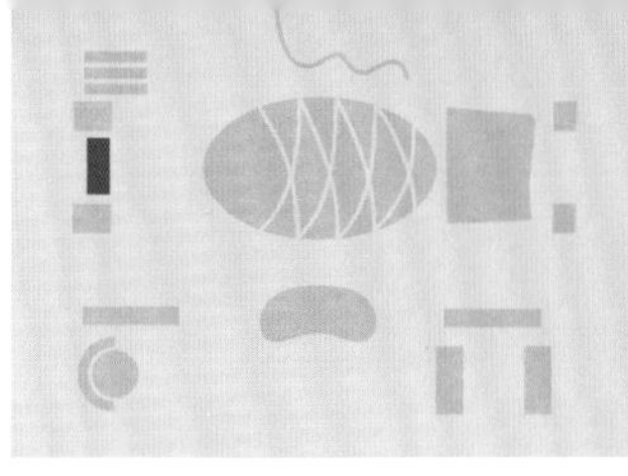

Harris Theater

It's a machine for making music.

—THOMAS BEEBY

Joan Harris first considered the idea of creating a new theater shared by a dozen performance groups in 1978, when she was on the board of directors for the Chicago Opera Theater, one of many accomplished local groups that did not have a decent venue in which to present its work. Unlike theatrical groups that can make do in a raw loft with bleacher seats and actors who know how to project, musicians are handicapped in a space without good acoustics, and dancers are hobbled if sight lines are obstructed and the floor is imperfect. With the creation of Millennium Park, the Joan W. and Irving B. Harris Theater for Music and Dance became a reality at last.

Harris, who paid $39 million of the theater's nearly $53 million cost and is chair of the Chicago foundation named for her husband, Irving Harris, teamed with Sandra Guthman, president and CEO for her family's Polk Brothers Foundation. Responsibilities were divided between them, with Harris overseeing architecture and Guthman working on financing. They came close to realizing their dream twice before their theater finally went to Millennium Park. Sites had been selected, and, on one of them, construction had actually begun. By 1999 Harris was ready to abandon the idea as unworkable. She and Guthman were figuring out how to return the millions of dollars donors had given. Then things changed.

At last

Ed Uhlir, recently hired to oversee all aspects of Millennium Park, had been taking a hard look at the park's master plan in 1999, and he saw possibilities others had not. For one, he noticed that the outdoor pavilion—not yet the Gehry-designed Pritzker Pavilion—included a proposed three-hundred-seat, below-ground rehearsal hall. "It didn't make sense," Uhlir said. The facility could be a year-round, revenue-producing theater if it were enlarged. Event attendees would park in the garage below the park, making money for the City of Chicago.

Uhlir asked the architects at Skidmore, Owings & Merrill (SOM), who created the park's master plan, to upgrade the rehearsal hall to a full theater. They said it could not be done. Uhlir got a better idea. Not wanting to raise false hopes in Harris and Guthman, he called architect Thomas Beeby first. Beeby, a principal at Hammond Beeby Rupert Ainge Architects, had been working with Joan Harris on the music and dance theater through its many iterations. Could Beeby squeeze his theater into the spot designated for the rehearsal hall? Uhlir asked. It was a Friday, and he wanted Beeby's answer Monday.

Beeby was probably the only person who could provide an answer in that time frame. His office had gone so far as to develop construction drawings for the theater at the Ogden slip site and had completed advanced concept drawings for an unlikely notion to convert a Loop parking garage into the theater. (Beeby's office did figure that one out, and it proved strangely relevant later in the project.) Nobody knew the program requirements for the theater better than Beeby.

With its 1,525 seats and elaborate stage support facilities that include a seventy-five-foot-tall fly tower, the Harris Theater auditorium is at least five times larger than the rehearsal hall originally proposed by SOM for the same site. Beeby knew construction would be difficult. The park stands on a constructed deck, the ground below it is landfill, and the theater site is hemmed in on all sides by other structures. But Beeby agreed that a full theater, rather than a rehearsal hall, was possible. He did not have the time to develop the section drawing, but he nevertheless told Uhlir that the idea would work.

In one stroke, Uhlir had pulled together a deal that shifted almost all the construction costs for the planned rehearsal hall away from the city, produced parking income for the city, and gave the theater a home. (Because of its independent funding, the theater is the only part of Millennium Park that does not belong to the city. It is an independent organization residing on property leased to it by the city.) With audiences virtually guaranteed—all the subscribers of the dozen pioneer groups were sure to go to the new facility—the theater also promised that one corner of Millennium Park would be actively populated, the true measure of success for any public space. As it turned out, getting people to come to the park would not be a problem, but at that early date, no one knew how popular the park would prove to be.

When they heard of the new location, Guthman was ecstatic, but Harris was more reserved. John Bryan persuaded her that it would work to both their advantages. The inclusion of a year-round indoor theater clearly enriched the park culturally. The theater presented attractive fund-raising possibilities among Bryan's private donors; the people who had refused to give money for a public park might feel differently about a theater. Bryan and Harris collaborated on one money-raising effort to more than a dozen potential donors and split the proceeds between Millennium Park and the theater.

Insurance

Before the theater could be built, however, another daunting worry would have to be addressed. With more than a century-old history of both protecting the lakefront as open parkland accessible to every citizen (the city's most valuable real estate is not on the tax rolls) and, contrarily, tolerating massive built incursions there such as McCormick Place and the water filtration plant, Chicago had accumulated many lawsuits and three relevant Illinois Supreme Court decisions about the lakefront. As it unfolded, that history inspired a corresponding organizing movement of vigilant, vigorous, citizen defenders of lakefront parks. Legal precedents and citizens have brought an imperfect, pugnacious sliding balance to the lakefront.

Specifically at issue for the Harris Theater were the Illinois Supreme Court rulings made between 1897 and 1911 that relied on an 1836 map with a notation on the spot where the city met the lake—in the days before landfill—at Michigan Avenue. The map, made by three state commissioners, read, "Public Ground—A Common to Remain Forever, Open, Clear and Free of any Buildings or Obstruction Whatever." Based on that, the court's rulings consistently forbade buildings on the lakefront between Randolph and what is now Roosevelt Road (earlier it was known as Twelfth Street). Could those rulings stop the Harris Theater from going into Millennium Park? The project would not advance until the theater's sponsors knew.

"I don't normally push my husband, but he is the best real estate lawyer in Chicago," Sandra Guthman said of her husband, Jack. She is not alone in that opinion; Jack Guthman is known for getting things done. There were times in the past when Jack Guthman and Uhlir, who worked in various roles for the Chicago Park District for years, were on opposite sides "throwing darts at each other," as Jack Guthman said. In this case, though, Jack Guthman was with the city. He had already worked on the plan approved by the city's Planning Commission for Millennium Park. But that plan had not included any buildings. (The music pavilion was part of the original plan, but it did not count, legally, as a building.) Now, a revised plan including the theater would have to be approved by the city.

4
4 UPPER LOBBY
3 UPPER BALCONY
2 LOWER BALCONY
1 ORCHESTRA

Guthman came up with a strategy that he thought might work. Museums are exceptions to the Illinois Supreme Court rulings; they are permitted on the lakefront under certain circumstances. The Art Institute of Chicago, as the best-known standing exemption to the court rulings and Millennium Park's closest neighbor, would provide the model.

"Museums keep everything," Guthman said. He thought the Art Institute would still have records dating back to 1891 showing how it got permission to build in a lakefront park. He found letters sent by the Art Institute to all the neighboring property owners to sign giving the museum permission to build in the park. By copying the wording of the Art Institute waivers and obtaining signed consent from owners who would be the Harris Theater's neighbors, Guthman would have a strong legal precedent on his side when the city was asked to approve a revised plan with the Harris Theater as a part of it.

Uhlir needed to make individual presentations to adjacent property owners. The group included some organizations not known for reasonable, predictable decision making, such as condominium associations, but he persuaded all of them to sign. With Beeby along to explain the theater's design, Uhlir also made presentations to key public-interest and park advocates' groups. Arguably, all that was required was a substantial majority of the neighbors as signers, but after all they had been through, Sandra Guthman and Joan Harris—and Jack Guthman too—wanted consensus. Jack Guthman warned Uhlir that Uhlir would never get the watchdog group Friends of the Parks to endorse the theater.

Beeby knew the rules governing the lakefront, and he knew better than to bring a design for a five-story theater to Friends of the Parks. His team found it could get the building into the volume it had been given in the park by shoehorning three of the theater's five stories below ground. Beeby did not want to go any deeper because that would put a portion of the building below lake level, immediately increasing the project's costs and complexity. The scheme Beeby showed was for a two-story building—with the three underground levels invisible from the street—in a streamlined, classical style meant to complement SOM's original Beaux Arts master plan.

When Friends of the Parks president Erma Tranter asked for all but the entry to the theater to go below ground, Beeby and Uhlir were not especially surprised. "We kept getting pushed further and further down," Beeby said ruefully. Beeby and Uhlir agreed to Tranter's request. Beeby would have to redesign the theater again.

More delays

The city, with its goal of completing the park by the year 2000 still in place at that time, was under pressure to begin construction. Uhlir, Beeby, and the theater's supporters were winning the approvals they needed, but it was taking time. And the cost was rising as the theater sank farther below the street. "Always the money," Beeby said, sighing. Could the sponsors raise all they needed? It came to a point: should caissons be sunk to support a parking garage or a theater? A decision had to be made and work had to start to prevent other parts of the park from being delayed. In the amount of time they had been given, the architects could not get working drawings finished before the deadline. The city proceeded with the parking garage foundations. If the theater happened, it would be left to the architect to adapt the parking garage supports to a theater. Beeby's peculiar exercise for the Loop garage renovation was not irrelevant after all.

The juggling act over the foundation was not that unusual. Trying to keep the project moving forward in advance of formal approvals and financing, Uhlir reassured the architect and the funders that it would work out. Conversations over who would pay for the foundations—the city or the theater—continued amicably after the foundations were in place. When the financing package was incomplete as the starting date for construction approached, Irving Harris stepped in to make a $6.3 million loan. (Irving Harris lived to see the theater bearing his and his wife's name open on November 8, 2003, but died not long after, at the age of ninety-four, on September 25, 2004.) In the end, the city paid for the foundations, and the Harris loan was repaid.

When the amended plan for Millennium Park—including the Harris Theater—went to the city's Planning Commission, just two people showed up to speak in opposition. The plan was approved. But Jack Guthman, ever cautious, was still not satisfied; he arranged for a test case. He enlisted a couple (friends of his from college) who were also residents of a building near Millennium Park to file a lawsuit protesting the theater's approval by the city. "We sued ourselves," said Beeby. It went to trial, and a judge, basing his decision on the Art Institute case, ruled in the city's and the theater's favor.

The new design

Although a substantial amount of Beeby's work is historically influenced—take, for example, the Chicago Public Library on State and Congress (1991)—the Harris, with its decidedly modern and functionalist air, demonstrates that Beeby is not in thrall to one aesthetic. The evolution of the Harris Theater illustrates the same point: Beeby responded to the context and program; every time the theater's site changed, so did the architectural style. His fluency in different design styles makes Beeby an architect's architect; his willingness to investigate and adapt his architectural designs makes him a client's architect.

"We wanted to design it from the inside out," Joan Harris said. "There were ground rules." The sponsors—not the architect—would select and hire the acoustician. Harris said Beeby understood that "when it came to a choice between architecture and acoustics, I would come down on the side of acoustics." More than anything, Harris wanted an architect who would listen, be personally committed to the project, and not view the theater as an exercise in architectural ego building.

The vision for the design was articulated by Harris. She wanted what she called "a performance machine." What she meant by that was a theater with all the contemporary technical support provided—loading docks and elevators for moving large scenery, a sprung floor for dancers, perfect acoustics for music—and nothing extra. (It could be argued that the scrupulous attention given to the performers left the audience shortchanged in one respect: accessibility. Beeby is working to remedy that by providing access to more elevators for those who either cannot or do not want to climb as many as three long flights of stairs to the street level after performances.) What money the sponsors had would go to maximizing the theater's performance features. Sandra Guthman said, "We didn't have money for marble." The theater would be mutable, its identity changing with each performance. Its strengths come out as called upon. For dance, the unobstructed sight lines take precedence; for live music, the acoustics are the thing.

Beeby took Harris's pared-down design brief to heart. Everything about the theater is minimal and unadorned. Indeed, Beeby said he took it as a compliment when his longtime friend, the architect Larry Booth, sized up the building, saying, "It looks like you're at a hockey game and then you find there's an opera going on inside."

Harris contrasted her vision with Chicago's 1904 Orchestra Hall: "I know when I walk up to that building that it says something. It says, 'We've been here for one hundred years and we offer the best of white European culture.'" That is not the impression Harris wanted to convey in the new theater. "We have a serially integrated audience. If there is Mexican dance, there are a lot of flounced skirts [in the audience]; when Merce Cunningham [dance company] is here, everybody is in black jeans and shirts; for Music of the Baroque, you see lots of white hair."

Beeby would have preferred a more visible design, but he understood that was not an option. More than most people, architects want their work to be noticed. Unlike most architects, however, Beeby is modest. Still, the challenges were considerable. Building below ground is more expensive; at its lowest point, the theater would stand thirty-four feet below lake level. There would be the additional cost of a system to keep water from seeping into the building. Hemmed in on all four sides by other structures, the theater's volume would be tightly constrained, making construction difficult. To the east of the Harris is the city's parking garage; to the west is a below-ground dedicated bus lane; the supports that elevate Randolph Street lie to the north, and to the south is Gehry's Pritzker Pavilion, which shares some facilities with the Harris.

The steel frame structure Beeby's team designed provided the strength and rigidity needed to clear the 152-foot span of the performance hall without intermediary support columns that would block sight lines. Using horizontal bridging elements to connect to the vertical supports for the city's parking garage, the architects could make a mat evenly distributing the weight of their building over the entire foundation. To keep water from leaching into the building, the architects designed two walls encircling the site penetrating down through the foundation level. Pumps between the walls automatically eliminate any water penetrating the outer wall before the second wall can be breached. Sheet piling—the term for this construction feature—is conventional in high-rise construction where the weight of the building is enormous and foundations must go deep. It is extremely rare in a building the size of the Harris, and it was necessary purely because of the site on landfill and the constraints on building above ground. Building below lake level also meant water's buoyant force would be pushing the building upward from below. That force would have to be counterbalanced structurally. Known as reverse hydrostatic pressure, this effect is something engineers can and do regularly compensate for in their calculations. As long as the upward pressure is consistent, the building is stable.

With architects like Frank Gehry winning commissions in the park, the Beaux Arts master plan was no longer the dominant design driver it had been. Beeby moved away from the classical vocabulary for his new design. On Randolph Street, the theater's presence would be announced by a small glass entry pavilion designed to look as light and airy as a greenhouse. It was a modern design with a hint at historical forms suggested in its vaulted roofline. The scheme was approved, and the architects finished the working drawings used for construction.

Then there was another setback. Between completing the drawings and starting construction, the cost of American steel rose a precipitous 20 percent. In one blow, the

project's budget was demolished. There was no possibility of substituting cheaper foreign steel; according to local requirements, only domestic steel can be used in projects on city-owned property. Suddenly Beeby found himself looking at yet another round of design and construction drawings—the third complete, detailed design he had done for the theater. He could redesign just as soon as he could figure out an affordable structural material that would be suitable for the theater. Whatever the material was, it would have to match the strength of steel to make the long, unsupported spans in the auditorium.

Construction manager Richard Halpern, chair of the Rise Group, came up with the solution. He suggested using the massive prefabricated concrete supports customarily employed in highways. Named for their shapes, the principal elements used in the Harris Theater are called "bulb-ts" and "double-ts." Inexpensive and incredibly strong, these supports gave Beeby the spans he needed. Enormous factory-made concrete panels—some as long as forty feet—were used as finished walls. Working with such enormous building components reduced the overall number of joints and connections throughout the building, simplifying design and construction. Beeby said, "In some ways the detailing was easier because there were fewer possibilities." For the entry pavilion, Beeby wanted to retain the purity of the steel scheme. Indeed, he would simplify it even more over time.

The guiding principles

Through the various designs, the principles shaping the auditorium remained the same. The acoustics and sight lines were of primary importance. In most theaters, the seats in the back half of the hall are inferior. But the Harris, Beeby said, was "designed to provide good seats in a democratic way." That translated into having no boxes and raking the seats in the back half of the hall more steeply than is typical so people sitting there could see everything—including the dancers' feet on the stage—over the heads of those in front of them. With its nearly square shape and three distinct and equal seating zones—front, back and balcony—the hall has an elastic quality. Even when it is less than half filled, it feels substantially occupied.

Simple black metal towers on either side of the stage support lights and the acoustical reflectors that direct sound to the back of the hall. Mark Holden, a principal at JaffeHolden Acoustics, promised Harris he personally would work on the theater. Working closely with Harris and with Beeby, he designed a beautiful light-colored wooden collapsible shell and ceiling for the stage that is moved into place for musical performances. When the building was finished, Holden went with Harris to tune the hall. They took seats in the auditorium, and a trumpeter played three notes from the stage: Holden turned to Harris and said there was nothing he could do to make it better—it was perfect. Harris must have known that because she was already crying.

The tight site conditions required an unusual approach. Typically, it is most efficient to have trade groups—the precast workers, for example—come on the site when they can start and complete their work. That would not be possible here. Starting with the back-of-the-house and performance areas, the building was completed in three stages. While construction on the back of the theater proceeded, the balance of the site was used to store materials and as a base for equipment. Materials were brought to the site mostly as needed. The crane was enormous. Positioned at the northwest corner of the site, it could reach diagonally to the far back corner of the auditorium, a distance of nearly 215 feet. The various trades were cycled in and out three times on cue to work on each phase. The process was more like building three buildings than one.

Theater as chameleon

The theater's aesthetic richness is subtly consistent with the very nature of theater and performance, in which absorbing experiences for audiences are conjured out of the most ephemeral and impermanent materials. Beeby used a staple of the theater, the intangible medium of light, to define and transform the public areas of his building. In homage to artist Dan Flavin, simple, inexpensive fluorescent-tube lighting has been mounted in graphic linear patterns throughout the public stairwell and lobbies of the theater. Most of these are white, but some emit colored light (each level has a different identifying color). At intermissions, the white lights are turned off and the colored lights are left on. This does not create the color-saturated environments Flavin did, but the effect is enlivening. The auditorium's curtain is similar conceptually. A custom-made piece by textile designer Maya Romanoff, the curtain is neutral to the point of being inert until it is lit and becomes mysteriously animated and beautiful.

The theatrical sensibility extends to the signature art piece at the theater entry, a Louise Nevelson–designed set piece from a 1984 production of the opera *Orfeo and Eurydice* at the St. Louis Opera. The piece was purchased by the Harrises and later donated to the Chicago Public Library, which, in turn, offered it to the theater on permanent loan. It is an enormous plywood panel, painted black with a grid and geometric forms applied across its surface in a contrasting gold color. A red, looping form—an abstracted lyre—dangles in front of the composition, the entirety of which is roughly made, as all stage sets are, from materials not at all precious.

The theater is marked on Randolph Street by a simple and elegant glass-and-concrete structure 40 feet tall (and, at 1,800 square feet, about the same size as a three-bedroom apartment; all told, the theater is 140,000 square feet) that serves as the building's formal entry and lobby. Brightly lit, it is also an integral marquee wordlessly signaling the theater's presence and beckoning attendees to its events. It has surprised planners with its effectiveness; theater attendees clearly prefer to enter not through the connected parking garage, as anticipated, but at the street level, where the approach is more inviting, more urbane, and, in its own modest way, more celebratory.

Standing behind Gehry's Pritzker Pavilion, the Harris Theater's rectilinear, understated entry is both a contrast and a relief to its flamboyant neighbor. The difference between the two buildings brings each into sharper focus and suggests the way in which cities are put together, a gradual process that over time brings different styles and scales of architecture together. The sense of control the Harris exudes is a good thing for Millennium Park, where exuberance is the rule. At the same time, the theater helps button down the vast openness along Randolph while engaging the AON Building across the way in conversation.

Just as Millennium Park is an urban park reinterpreted for the twenty-first century, the Harris is a performance space for a new age. From the original twelve, the theater grew to host thirty-eight performance companies in a recent season. Exceeding even Joan Harris's hopes, the theater entertains a melting-pot mix of ethnically and culturally diverse groups. Chameleon-like, the theater transforms itself with each performance to accommodate performers and audience. Like the best host, the Harris is devoted to its guests' pleasure.

Photograph Credits

Cover — James Steinkamp, Steinkamp Photography

Frontispiece — James Steinkamp, Steinkamp Photography **2**

Acknowledgments — James Steinkamp, Steinkamp Photography **8**

From Nothing: The Story of Millennium Park

Photographs by Peter Barreras (www.barrerasphoto.com) **11, 12, 14, 15, 17, 18, 22, 25, 28**
Photo © Linda Oyama Bryan for Gustafson Guthrie Nichol Ltd. **21**
Scott McDonald © Hedrich Blessing **13**
James Steinkamp, Steinkamp Photography **10, 16, 26**

Cloud Gate

Photographs by Peter Barreras (www.barrerasphoto.com) **31, 34, 35, 36, 37, 41, 44**
Scott McDonald © Hedrich Blessing **30, 39**
James Steinkamp, Steinkamp Photography **33, 38, 40, 43, 45, 46, 48**

Jay Pritzker Pavilion

Photographs by Peter Barreras (www.barrerasphoto.com) **53, 54, 55, 57, 58, 59, 61, 62, 63, 64, 65, 66, 67**
Scott McDonald © Hedrich Blessing **50, 51**
James Steinkamp, Steinkamp Photography **56**

BP Bridge

Photographs by Peter Barreras (www.barrerasphoto.com) **69, 70, 71, 72, 74, 75, 76, 78**
Scott McDonald © Hedrich Blessing **68**

Crown Fountain

Photographs by Peter Barreras (www.barrerasphoto.com) **81, 82, 84, 86, 87, 90, 92**
Steve Hall © Hedrich Blessing **89**
Scott McDonald © Hedrich Blessing **80**
James Steinkamp, Steinkamp Photography **83**

Exelon Pavilions

Photographs by Peter Barreras (www.barrerasphoto.com) **94, 95, 97**
Charles G. Young, Interactive Design Architects **96**

McDonald's Cycle Center

Photographs by Peter Barreras (www.barrerasphoto.com) **98, 99, 100, 101**

Lurie Garden

Photographs by Peter Barreras (www.barrerasphoto.com) **103, 116, 119, 120**
Photo © Linda Oyama Bryan for Gustafson Guthrie Nichol Ltd. **105, 106, 108, 111, 112, 113, 115, 117, 118**
James Steinkamp, Steinkamp Photography **102**

Millennium Monument at Wrigley Square

Photographs by Peter Barreras (www.barrerasphoto.com) **123**
Bob Harr © Hedrich Blessing **124**
Scott McDonald © Hedrich Blessing **122**

Boeing Galleries

Photographs by Peter Barreras (www.barrerasphoto.com) **126, 127, 128, 129**

Harris Theater

Hedrich Blessing **136**
Sasha Fornari **135**
Marianne Jankowski **131**
Liz Lauren **133, 138, 141, 143**
Jon Miller © Hedrich Blessing **130, 134, 144**